managed
moves

A complete guide to managed moves
as an alternative to permanent exclusion

ADAM ABDELNOOR

 CALOUSTE GULBENKIAN FOUNDATION

Published by
Calouste Gulbenkian Foundation
United Kingdom Branch
98 Portland Place
London W1B 1ET
Tel: 020 7908 7604
E-mail: info@gulbenkian.org.uk
Website: www.gulbenkian.org.uk

ISBN 9781 903080 07 8

British Library Cataloguing-in-Publication Data
A catalogue record for this book is available from the British Library

Designed by Andrew Shoolbred, cover designed by Helen Swansbourne
Printed by Expression Printers Ltd, IP23 8HH

Distributed by Central Books Ltd, 99 Wallis Road, London E9 5LN
Tel: 0845 458 9911, Fax: 0845 458 9912
E-mail: orders@centralbooks.com
Website: www.centralbooks.com

Contents

Preface

If the educational future of a pupil who is permanently excluded from school is not given sufficient thought or direction then the pupil is in a sense excluded twice: once from the school they attended, and again from the educational system itself. In these circumstances, the word 'permanent' may take on a particularly literal meaning: the student is permanently beyond the reach of a proper education and may be permanently, or at least severely, affected by it. Their life chances are likely to be damaged; they may drift into crime. It is noticeable that a significant proportion of young people in the criminal justice system have been permanently excluded from school.

'Managed moves', as the name suggests, offer permanently excluded pupils a carefully planned route back into education or what the author of this book describes as 'a plan for recovery'. In other words the system it espouses is ultimately inclusive and humane.

Managed moves, however, are not new. Since 2004 the then Department for Education and Skills has advocated their use as an alternative to permanent exclusion; and about one-third of local authorities now promote some form of 'managed move' in their schools. Invariably, the results are impressive. One local authority, for example, has succeeded in reducing its permanent exclusions from 68 to zero in two years. Other local authorities that have adopted the approach report not dissimilar success rates.

But if managed moves are to be effective they inevitably need to be carefully planned. A considerable number of different parties are involved in the process, and being alert to, and attempting to reconcile, their various needs can be a complex and demanding task. There is a danger that, if all the different aspects of a managed move are not properly attended to, the method will either fail or be only partially successful. This will not only rebound on the pupils and those others involved, it may also damage the reputation of the system itself and so discourage its wider use.

It was these considerations that prompted the Foundation to commission this guide – the first of its kind on the market – and to promote its use in schools and local authorities. We hope that it will play its part in both encouraging the wider take-up of this enlightened alternative to permanent exclusion, and in assisting those who have already begun to adopt the managed moves process.

Simon Richey
Assistant Director, Education
Calouste Gulbenkian Foundation (UK and Ireland Branch)

About this book

The methods described in this guide will be of use to anyone involved in school exclusions. That includes headteachers and senior managers; professionals who work with excluded or at-risk children; managers of children's services; and all those who would like to see the use of alternatives to exclusion. It is hoped that schools and education communities can use the guide to improve the quality of service provided to children who need to leave their current school and go to an alternative setting.

Part 1 sets the scene, explaining how managed moves work, what the advantages are and how the process compares with permanent exclusion.

Part 2 takes the schools' perspective, showing how movements around the education community can be carried out fairly and effectively, using a voluntary approach.

Part 3 is mainly for professionals who facilitate managed moves, and describes a tried and tested method which brings all parties together, and enables them to reach consensus, resolution, and a learning plan for the future.

Part 4 explores the wider picture for the whole education community. It raises issues for education managers who want to develop an area-wide strategy. It examines the fair use of education funds, ways to develop a greater range of alternative learning resources and of realising a common vision for this new approach within a community.

The case studies in this book are taken from real experiences although details have been altered and the names of individual children have been changed to protect their identity and welfare.

INTRODUCTION
TO MANAGED
MOVES

Chapter 1

AN ALTERNATIVE TO PERMANENT EXCLUSION

Jerry had made good progress at school until Year 9 when he became withdrawn and argumentative. He disliked writing and in Year 10 found it hard to keep up with the increased workload. As a result his attendance rate fell, and he began to lose his temper and storm out of class. He was a strong character and sometimes led other children astray. Although Jerry's tutor had a good relationship with him and was able to talk to him about his anxieties, other teachers were stressed by Jerry's truculence and the disruption his outbursts caused. The school tried different learning support strategies to help him. However, Jerry's family life also became difficult and he started staying over with friends when things were bad at home. The headteacher recognised that Jerry was not coping with the combined pressures of mainstream school and his home life. He was sympathetic to the situation, but also concerned for the teachers and other children who complained about his behaviour. He could see that an alternative learning programme was needed.

The headteacher contacted his local authority inclusion team who arranged school and home visits by a Managed Moves facilitator. The head told the facilitator that Jerry could stay in school if he made amends for his past behaviour and was able to keep to an agreement about future conduct. However, he was very sceptical indeed about Jerry's ability to do so. Jerry was initially opposed to the idea of moving elsewhere, but the facilitator encouraged him to talk about what he liked to learn and what he hoped to do when he left school. Jerry didn't really know, but he did say he wanted to work out of doors and with his hands. She was able to offer him an alternative programme based at the local Pupil Referral Unit (PRU) for three days a week, with one day a week spent in college on a vocational course. The PRU had developed links with the local office of the National Trust and she thought he might be able to obtain work experience with the maintenance team of a nearby country house for one day a week. Jerry agreed to visit the PRU and talk to the teachers there. The visit went well but Jerry was still reluctant to go there, and his father in particular was dismayed that he might 'miss out and never get any qualifications'. The facilitator was able to explain to Jerry and his father the diversity of pathways to qualification that are now available, and helped them both to see how difficult things were at Jerry's current school and to understand the probability of permanent exclusion.

At a managed move conference attended by the headteacher, the head of the PRU and Jerry and his parents, the facilitator made sure the discussion was very realistic. Jerry was offered a real choice between keeping to the agreement about his future conduct in order to stay in school or taking up the new programme based at the PRU. At first, Jerry insisted that he could keep to the agreement, but as others round the table, including his parents, pointed out how tough it would be, and how much the new programme suited him, Jerry decided he would like to make the move. A short agreement to this effect was drawn up and all parties signed it.

Because Jerry had made a choice about his future he felt more positive about making the move. His attendance was excellent, and his characteristic determination helped him to achieve an ASDAN gold award based on his work experience, four GCSEs, and the offer of a trainee placement with the National Trust when he left college.

What are managed moves?

When pupils are permanently excluded from school a letter from the local education authority informs them where their future education will take place. However, they are not party to this decision. The most likely outcome is a place in a Pupil Referral Unit (PRU), though simply offering a child an alternative setting does not mean they will participate and it does not address the totality of their needs. Furthermore, the permanent exclusion process ignores both the children's and parents' views and all the sensitive information about their situation which could help uncover hidden needs. Even if the child is offered a place in another school, as sometimes happens, they will arrive at the school bearing the stigma of exclusion and teachers may be resistant to their inclusion.

Managed moves are an alternative to permanent exclusion. They enable a child or young person to make amends and to move on to a new placement or programme in a planned way which satisfies the school, the child and family and any individual who has been aggrieved. The process is designed to bring everyone involved together to find a solution, rather than simply to punish and blame.

Managed moves are highly flexible and admit far more possibilities than permanent exclusion. The main options could include: reconciliation and a fresh start at the current school; transfer to a new school or college, possibly with an adjusted learning programme; part-time school attendance with an individual learning and therapeutic programme elsewhere; full-time attendance at a PRU followed by a return to the current school or move to a new school or college; part-time attendance at a PRU combined with a home and community learning plan; or a home-based learning programme tailored to a child's special needs.

In arranging a managed move schools should be able to draw on the resources of the whole community to provide additional education settings, for example, learning at home, community-based options, voluntary agency support and/or specialist input such as drugs support.

Unlike exclusion, a managed move is a voluntary agreement made between:
- A pupil and his or her parents or carers.[1]
- The school from which the child may move.
- The person with responsibility for providing or coordinating the individual education plan (IEP) the pupil is being offered – this could be the headteacher of a school receiving the child, or of a PRU, or a community practitioner who is managing a programme uniquely designed for that child.

This new approach answers the question 'If we do not want to use exclusion, how should the school manage children whose place here is no longer viable?' We don't ask 'Should we exclude this pupil?' but 'How can we, as a community, find a place for this pupil and their particular learning needs?'

When can managed moves be used?
The managed move process may be initiated when:
- Relationships between child and school have broken down completely.
- The child is unhappy at the school and refuses to attend.
- The child has seriously contravened school rules.
- The child is putting other children at risk of harm.
- A child with additional personal or social needs makes little or no educational progress in the current setting.
- The child has social and developmental needs the school cannot meet.

If the school decides a child cannot remain there, the first priority should be to organise a managed move to ensure the child has the best chance of remaining within safe, supervised surroundings for the length of the school day, of learning better social skills and of achieving to the best of their ability. This will be much easier for the community to accomplish if the child has not experienced the rejection of permanent exclusion. However, even if a permanent exclusion has already been given, using a managed move with it should still be the top priority.

---

1   Throughout this book, 'parent' means parent, adult family member or other carer.

Managed moves can work both ways

Because managed moves are voluntary, there is no statutory restriction on their use. Furthermore, the same management process can be used to integrate children from alternative education *into* mainstream and to broker the inclusion of a pupil with physical and/or intellectual disabilities.

What are the advantages?

Generally, people find the managed move process easier, kinder and more educationally effective than permanent exclusion. Where used, it is radically reducing rates of permanent exclusion. Managed moves are forward-looking instead of retrospective and provide a plan for recovery, whereas permanent exclusion offers no forward plan.

Managed moves create the context for therapeutic and systematic intervention. Children and parents feel they still have a role in deciding what comes next, and the process can draw out previously unknown issues and give services the opportunity to respond to these positively.

From both the children's and the families' points of view, instead of rejection the focus is on finding a solution, and all parties are included in the process.

For schools, it creates a more positive ethos, placing the emphasis on what pupils are doing right rather than what they are doing wrong.

The managed move process

If a child can no longer remain in a school, a managed move needs to be arranged between the current school and a place of education that will provide an alternative learning offer that better meets their educational, social and emotional learning needs.

The key participants in the managed move process are:

- Representatives of the current education setting.
- Representatives of the proposed new education setting.
- The child and their parents or carers.
- Other concerned agencies.
- A managed moves facilitator.

Managed moves are achieved through a series of individual meetings and discussions with each of the key participants followed by a restorative justice conference, at which everyone's views and concerns are brought together, people listen to each other, and an alternative education plan which meets the needs of all key participants is agreed voluntarily. This agreement should be seen as binding even though the process is voluntary.

The plan which a child and his parents may be offered can cover agreements about schooling (including community and online learning), and psychosocial, welfare and youth justice interventions; and include clauses that agree different outcomes depending upon how well the child is able to keep their side of the bargain.

Restorative justice is a key principle for managed moves. It offers an approach which makes the wrong-doer accountable, in a supported way, and avoids the mine-fields of 'charge sheets', 'evidence', 'prosecution' and 'judgement'. It is just like justice for a small island, or, more accurately, justice for a community of island schools. It enables the wrong-doer to make reparations, and for injured parties to be heard and receive apologies or compensation. It is then easier for everyone to move on.

The headteacher has a crucial role in deciding how and when managed moves are used, and will need to involve the governors so that this voluntary process can work alongside mandatory permanent exclusions guidance.

Thinking about the child who has offended

Children at risk of exclusion are generally educationally disadvantaged by 'social and relational disability' – that is their relationships tend to be dysfunctional. Such disabil-ity is usually associated with social deprivation, poor parenting and nurturing, serious developmental needs and specific disorders such as autism. The classroom, the play-ground, the headteacher's office and the exclusions appeals panel are all settings where children with very poor social and relational skills, and their families, are likely to perform badly. The method described in this book creates an environment which compensates for these difficulties as much as possible.

But it is not realistic to argue that children can stay in class no matter what – sometimes relations within a school break down completely. Then, alternatives to mainstream education can still provide an opportunity for a young person to develop in ways that meet their needs better than their school can. There are also times when the needs of the majority of children and staff in a school outweigh the needs of an individual.

Changing the dynamic

In the safe, supervised surroundings of school, we are in a position both to confront and to try to understand behaviour which causes social harm. That is why the act of exclusion, which rejects people, breaks social links and risks losing the child to the streets, is unhelpful. It takes the child out of a context in which we can engage with them, intervene and help. It also marginalises the child and their family, which can trigger more resentment and antisocial behaviour.

If possible, we should try to ensure that pupils have a choice, are supported and have been listened to. This is the best way to ensure they have listened themselves, and have had a fair chance to succeed to the best of their abilities. *Managed Moves* explains how this may be achieved by doing everything possible to keep a child within the school, or by doing everything possible to keep them in an alternative educative setting.

This is not 'do-gooding'. It is about reducing social harm, which has a real cost to all of us, whether in taxes or in a poorer quality of life in the community. When we reverse the dynamic of exclusion (rejection *from* the community) and create a bridge *to* an alternative offer, we hold on to the child, help to forge new links and bring people together positively. A successful managed move leads the child to safe supervised surroundings where their *educational, social and developmental needs* are addressed. This will reduce youth offending and antisocial behaviour, and subsequent problems such as crime, suicide, dysfunctional relationships and an inability to engage with the world of work.

Permanent exclusion, as its name implies, can be a permanent solution to a temporary problem. Many children passing through a turbulent adolescent phase may have their education disrupted, and relationships with adults and friends forcibly terminated as a result of permanent exclusion. A 1993 study found that two-thirds of disruptive children spontaneously settle down and stop being a problem.[2]

Do children sometimes choose exclusion?

It is ironic that if a child chooses not to attend school, procedural and legal steps are taken to make them do so, but if a child behaves badly enough they can provoke an exclusion. It must give them some satisfaction to receive from the school a letter which, among other things, instructs them never to come to the school again.

On more than one occasion headteachers have reported that within hours of receiving a final warning the child concerned has repeated the behaviour. This amounts to self-exclusion.

When this happens schools sometimes assume that 'the problems were more serious than we thought' – that the child was not in control of their actions. If we assume they are, then their behaviour becomes rational. Children who 'seek a way out' feel that they cannot cope with or succeed in the education community.

Outside the care and supervision of school, they are likely to join others like themselves, miss out on essential opportunities and be drawn into illegal activities. That is why the community needs to find ways to hold on to these children, rather than pushing them away.

The needs of those who are aggrieved

Although the managed move process has been established to address the needs of those in danger of exclusion, it also prioritises the needs of those who are *aggrieved*. Conventional justice sets victims to one side in its pursuit of judgement and sanctions. This is true in the application of school codes as well as in the law courts.

Restorative justice makes wrong-doers accountable for their actions and gives the aggrieved an opportunity to ask the questions which may be plaguing them – usually starting with 'Why did you do it?' – in a safe and carefully managed environment.

---

2   K. Topping, *Educational Systems for Disruptive Adolescents* (London, Croom Helm, 1993).

The aggrieved have an opportunity to vent their feelings to the wrong-doer (in an appropriate way and with support). There is the chance for them to ask for and hear reassurances about the wrong-doers' contrition, to ask for and receive reparation, and, where possible, for true reconciliation to follow. This applies whether the aggrieved is a pupil or a teacher.

The managed move process is the lever by which wrong-doers are made accountable for their actions, and provides the context for the positive results of a restorative conference: reparation, reconciliation, closure and a forward plan to which all can commit.

Whether the pathway chosen is a managed move or a permanent exclusion with a managed move, the restorative process produces better outcomes. In some ways this is the best reason of all to apply its principles to critical situations in school.

Some facts and figures about exclusion

Permanent exclusion is harmful to vulnerable children and families even though schools may find it necessary. There is abundant evidence that permanent exclusion inflicts further social harm on those who are already experiencing it, and almost universal agreement that it has a deleterious effect on childhood development into adulthood.[3]

Causes:
- Home Office research confirms 'the extreme social and educational disadvantage present in the backgrounds of young people who experience permanent exclusion'.[4]
- In research commissioned by the Children's Society to examine school exclusion from the perspective of families and children, eight out of ten parents said that their children had underlying needs that triggered the exclusion. One in three parents thought they themselves were seen as part of the problem by the school. More than half the children were said to have had special needs identified. A further one in five parents said their children found it hard to learn. Parents felt worried, upset and angry about the exclusion, and thought the process was unfair.[5]

Consequences:
- Enduring harm to children's educational development can follow from as short a period out of school as two weeks.[6]

---

3   Social Exclusion Unit, *Truanting and Exclusion* (London, HMSO, 2001).
4   D. Berridge, I. Brodie, *et al.*, *The independent effects of permanent exclusion from school in the offending careers of young people*. Home Office, RDS Occasional Paper No. 71 (London, HMSO, 2001).
5   C. Hayden and S. Dunne, *Outside, Looking In: Children's and families' experiences of exclusion from school* (London, Children's Society, 2001).
6   D. Kelly, 'Education and Difficult Children', in *Young Minds Magazine*, 29, 1997.

- More than three-quarters of young homeless teenagers are either long-term non-attenders or have been excluded from school.[7]
- Excluded children commit up to 50 per cent more offences in the year after exclusion than in the year leading up to it.[8]
- Eighty-three per cent of boys in the criminal justice system have been excluded.[9] More than 60 per cent of prisoners have been permanently excluded from school at some point, compared to less than 0.2 per cent of the wider population.[10]

Research shows managed or planned exclusion and reintegration can have success-ful outcomes, if appropriate support is available. Alternative education for children out of school is a key factor in breaking the link between exclusion, non-school atten-dance and offending.[11]

Government policy

The government is convinced that school exclusion should be avoided if possible. It has identified three key objectives: preventing those at special risk from becoming excluded, reintegrating those who have been excluded and improving basic service standards so that they are more inclusive.[12]

In 2004 the then Department for Education and Skills issued guidelines encour-aging schools to try managed moves as an alternative to permanent exclusion. Their guidance specifies two criteria: the move must be voluntary and it must be supported. It says:

'The headteacher may ask another headteacher to admit the pupil. This should only be done with the full knowledge and cooperation of all the parties involved, including the parents, governors and the local authority, and in circumstances where it is in the best interests of the pupil concerned. In order to fully address the pupil's difficulties it may be helpful for schools within an area to have a protocol in place [for managed moves] and to have a full support package in place for the pupil. Parents should never be pressured into removing their child from the school under threat of a permanent exclusion, nor should pupils' names be deleted from the school roll on disciplinary

7   Social Exclusion Unit, *Rough Sleeping* (London, Cabinet Office, 1998), p. 5.
8   Audit Commission Report, *Misspent Youth: Young people and crime* (London, Audit Commission, 1996).
9   M. Challen and T. Walton, *Juveniles in Custody: A unique insight into the perceptions of young people held in Prison Service custody in England and Wales* (London, Her Majesty's Inspectorate of Prisons, 2004).
10 Berridge, Brodie, *et al.*, see note 4.
11 Social Exclusion Unit, see note 3.
12 Social Exclusion Unit, *Preventing Social Exclusion* (London, HMSO, 1998).

grounds unless the formal permanent exclusion procedures set out in statute and in this guidance have been adhered to.'[13]

There is a third prerequisite: the managed move should be facilitated by someone impartial.

This ensures that managed moves are done in a fair and transparent way to meet the needs of the child. And because managed moves are voluntary, the learning objectives and individual education strategy must be planned for, delegated and accepted before the transfer can be agreed. The independent facilitator will have the skills and the time to follow through on the process as it develops; schools often have neither.

Government support for managed moves has created an opportunity to replace permanent exclusions with a process which is voluntary, restorative, and more effective. But if managed moves are carried out poorly, and especially if they are unfair, there is the danger of a backlash which could discourage their use. The critical challenge is to build capacity for managed moves which are fair, transparent, supportive and truly voluntary.

Current practice

A preliminary survey suggests that the approach is popular with schools and education communities which have tried it.[14]

About one-third of all local authorities are encouraging the use of some form of managed move following guidance from the DCSF. Some have been supporting managed moves since 2000. However, there appears to be no national strategy for regulating the process, and there is no national record of the number of managed moves that are taking place.

Individual local authorities report swingeing reductions in permanent exclusion rates where managed moves are used. Stoke-on-Trent reduced their secondary exclusions from 73 to 16 in one year (2003–4). Slough local authority reduced permanent exclusions in 2003–4 to seven (about a third of the national average), using a restorative managed transfer process, and a 'revolving door' approach to reintegration. Norfolk local authority reported that in the same year 39 of 45 possible permanent exclusions were replaced by managed moves. In North Lincolnshire there have been no permanent exclusions in the last two years (2004–6).

Recent research by Inaura the inclusion charity (see page 111) suggests that between 3,000 and 6,000 managed moves took place in 2006. Headteachers were

---

13 http://www.teachernet.gov.uk/wholeschool/behaviour/exclusion/guidance/part1/ (last accessed August 2007). Statutory guidance on exclusions changes regularly. Information on the current legal framework for exclusions is available on the government education website http://www.teachernet.gov.uk/wholeschool/behaviour/exclusion/guidance/ (last accessed August 2007).

14 A. Abdelnoor and P. Pisavadia, *Preliminary Assessment of Educational Managed Moves in England and Wales* (London, Inaura the inclusion charity, 2004).

asked to comment on their experience of the process. Their comments reveal a wide range of attitudes to managed moves matched by a wide range of interpretations of what the term means. The most consistent thread is the recognition that support (for the student and for the schools involved) and matching funding are essential. Head-teachers were more positive where community level (local authority) agreements were in place and there was a sense of shared ownership of the process. Some heads cited as issues a lack of training for schools, the absence of community level agree-ments and central coordination, and an insufficient range of alternative provision. They wanted to know that there was consistency across schools, an equitable distri-bution of managed moves and resources, and that the process is not simply being used as an easy option.

The impact of exclusions on human and financial resources

The direct cost of administering a permanent exclusion is in the region of £1,000.[15] This takes into account the staff time required, both in and out of school, to imple-ment the exclusion within DCSF regulations.

A managed move costs about £500 assuming about 10 hours of work by the facilitator and the involvement of a school representative (usually the headteacher).[16] Since the process is voluntary and the facilitator delivers the whole package, there is less administration and more core time spent listening and negotiating with all parties to establish the best route forward.

With permanent exclusion, indirect and time costs are much more liable to mount up. These include:

- Staff time to write reports for the 'exclusions dossier'.
- Senior management time spent preparing the exclusion documents for the local authority (this can be considerable).
- Governor and senior management time spent in hearing the parents' appeal, which often follows a permanent exclusion.
- Time and stress when parents request an independent appeal.

Local cooperation

Every local authority funds special needs and alternative education differently. Local authorities are free to restructure their funding policies and practice regularly. This freedom of action is an opportunity for authorities to develop innovative good prac-tice, but it also means that funding arrangements for the alternative sector can be too pragmatic and unfocused.

---

15 Calculation based on Table 6.2 of C. Parsons, *Education, Exclusion and Citizenship* (London, Routledge, 1999). With thanks to David Boyle, New Philanthropy Capital, London.

16 Working knowledge based on approximately 100 managed moves conducted by the author between 1995 and 2005.

The idea of education communities is to be encouraged. An education community can be seen as combining a cluster of schools, voluntary agencies and other organisations with common interests who share resources and work together to meet the needs of children and the community in a way that is fair to all parties. There are wide variations in the degree to which particular localities can be thought of as education communities. Unitary authorities are a good size. Large local authorities could be broken down into area communities. But what distinguishes a community of schools from a conglomeration of schools is that communality of interest and, in particular, shared activities and outcomes which bring them together.

2

MANAGED MOVES FROM THE SCHOOLS' PERSPECTIVE

Chapter 2

THE PRINCIPLES BEHIND MANAGED MOVES

This chapter describes the key values and operational criteria which apply to managed moves, and answers the most immediate questions which someone new to the subject might raise.

When a serious incident occurs in school it may not be immediately apparent that a voluntary approach is best. So when is a managed move appropriate and why is it almost always the preferred option? There are two fundamental issues: does the process give the school community the opportunity to express its disapproval of events which have led to the move, and is the move really voluntary if the only alternative is permanent exclusion? There is also the question of whether managed moves can completely replace permanent exclusion.

The voluntary nature of a managed move requires a different ethos from mandatory exclusion. In other words, exclusion happens *to* the pupil, whereas a managed move happens *with* the pupil.

Why is a managed move the preferred option?

- The restorative process is itself therapeutic. Although it may form the pathway to alternative education provision, it can also lead to a change within the school and the child which makes such a move unnecessary.
- Managed moves look to the future rather than to the past; they offer a plan for recovery. With permanent exclusions the child is not made accountable for their part in what has happened. A number of studies have shown that the aggrieved are less likely to experience post-traumatic stress symptoms if they have participated in a restorative process.[17]
- Once a managed move is agreed there is no need for an appeals procedure, which can drag on for months. But the process is still safeguarded. If the parents refuse a managed move, the school retains the right to exclude.
- Permanent exclusion always requires another management process to find the

---

17 For an example see http://www.realjustice.org/library/angel.html (last accessed August 2007).

child a new school or alternative provision, otherwise an educational vacuum follows, leading to more opportunities for delinquency and further social harm. It is more efficient and effective to have just one process linking the current and future settings.[18]

- Because the move is better managed, longer-term educational outcomes are likely to be better. Managed moves increase the likelihood of the child returning to a mainstream setting later (for instance, a college placement during Years 10 to 13). Alternative provision is more expensive than mainstream school, so managed moves are likely to save money.

Do managed moves completely replace permanent exclusion?
It is necessary both politically and practically for schools to retain the right to oblige a pupil to leave their community when this is essential. However, it is crucial to maintain a very clear dichotomy both in principle and practice between managed moves and permanent exclusion; otherwise there is a danger that the managed move process becomes voluntary in name only.

Shouldn't the punishment fit the crime?
Children are not asked to move because they have been 'bad' – problem behaviour only provides evidence that a need exists which may be better met elsewhere.

Where a serious incident has taken place headteachers often feel that a punishment is necessary. Some have said that even though a managed move means the child leaves the school, other pupils will see it as a soft option. The restorative approach allows schools to request reparation and atonement by the pupil, providing a good example for others.

Reparation
Reparation can take many forms including meeting with injured parties for mediation and apologies, financial reparation where appropriate, letters written to individuals or the school community which can be read out, or even a public apology before the whole school. It can also take the form of community service. Reparation can become part of the restorative negotiation and the school's agreement to a managed move could be contingent on it. The receiving school could do the same.

Contrast this with the absence of any apology or reparation following a permanent exclusion. Reparation will have a more positive effect on a school than rumours of exclusion and an assembly speech which will probably go unheard by those who are expected to benefit from it most.

---

18 Throughout this guide, 'current school' (or 'setting') means the establishment from which the managed move takes place and 'future school' (or 'setting') means the setting to which the child will go.

Key values and criteria

Four key values expedite successful outcomes in managed moves:

- Respect for equal opportunities
  ... because there must be a fair balance between the needs of the individual and the needs of the community.
- Attention to the needs of the whole person
  ... because the personal, social, emotional and psychological needs of the child are *always* factors contributing to exclusion from school.
- Promotion of choice and voluntary participation
  ... because we want to motivate the child in a new direction (not reject them). Voluntariness and motivation are closely linked. Even if the choices are limited, voluntary decisions are much more likely to be followed through.
- Appreciation and acceptance of feelings and opinions
  ... because if we want to expedite the 'whole person' needs and elicit their voluntary cooperation, we have to work *with* the child and family to appreciate, and show we appreciate, their sensitivities. We have to accept their imperatives, even if these seem odd or unprofessional, and be adaptable and flexible in our responses, without any collusion.

This guide identifies three core criteria to which all managed moves should aspire:

- Participation in a managed move is voluntary for all concerned.
- Managed moves are facilitated by someone impartial.
- They are supported by professional communities, family and friends.

A managed move is only voluntary if the pupil and parents give informed consent. The issues may be complex and they will need advice – most parents are not in a position to appreciate the organisational, educational or legal issues without help. Someone needs to be able to engage with all parties as an 'honest broker' and support and guide the child and parents who may be suspicious or confused.

An impartial facilitator can provide much-needed continuity throughout the process and monitor the support plan. Impartial here means 'someone not involved in the situation leading up to the managed move and not directly affected by the outcome'. It does not mean 'independent' in a legal sense.

Major changes in our lives are often challenging and stressful. For the child involved, a managed move is both, and the social developmental issues that made it an appropriate course of action still need to be addressed. Support before, during and after the move is essential, both for the child's emotional needs and to ensure that the additional (remedial) elements of the plan are understood and implemented.

The facilitator

The facilitator has a unique role in expediting a positive outcome for all parties. Ideally, this person should be skilled in interpersonal and group work, and in restorative justice approaches. Mature professionals will probably find it easier to win over parents, because they understand the challenge of parenting and have wider experience of working in a range of settings.

The facilitator 'lifts loads' – from the back of the headteacher and governors, and from the pupil and family. Acting as a go-between, and holding all the information from all parties, including some that was previously hidden or must remain confidential, the facilitator is well-placed to guide all parties towards a consensus on the best possible outcomes.

The local authority should be able to advise schools on the availability of a facilitator, who is normally one of the following:

- Someone provided by the local authority inclusion team.
- Somebody from a voluntary sector education agency tasked to do managed moves.
- Whoever normally deals with permanent exclusions in the local authority.

Schools might also ask the headteacher of the local PRU or the educational psychology service, the Social Services department, or the Youth Offending Team.

The lack of a trained facilitator need not be a barrier. Managed moves are still a relatively new idea and in some localities may not be resourced yet. In this case, a senior member of staff or special needs teacher with some of the required skills and time might be asked to take on this role.

Chapter 3

PLANNING STRATEGICALLY FOR MANAGED MOVES

The headteacher's role

Most headteachers have a sense of when the end of the road is in sight for a pupil in danger of exclusion. The managed move process allows them to recognise this explicitly, whilst leaving open the possibility of a change of direction, however unexpected.

A headteacher who is committed to the managed move process will allow it to unfold without resorting pre-emptively to permanent exclusion. A permanent exclusion always remains the final option and can be used if the managed move process fails.

Even if the headteacher has decided to permanently exclude without reservation, the managed move process can still be used to decide what should happen next.

The governors' role

Governors have oversight of permanent exclusions and so will become involved in the managed move process whenever it is taking place alongside a permanent exclusion process. Government policy on behaviour and exclusion is always being updated, and the mandatory requirements must take precedence. Luckily, managed moves are very flexible, and can adapt to different mandatory frameworks.

Making the child accountable

In an effective managed move process, the wrong-doer is made accountable for their actions. This is more likely to bring about positive changes than a permanent exclusion. It requires courage, and *lots of support*, for a young person to take personal responsibility for their actions. Without the restorative process, most children will feel that they've 'paid the price' through their punishment and no reparation is necessary.

When we support children in acting responsibly to 'put things right' with their community they experience how good that feels. The community's side of the bargain is providing a programme which will meet the child's needs, and which was designed *with the child's help*. These are very positive lessons with which to initiate the moving-on process. Children are unlikely to take responsibility unless they are really listened to.

What about parents' rights?

A great advantage in using a voluntary process is that it does not require a raft of procedural safeguards to protect parental or pupil rights. The mandatory process provides a fall-back position.

There is no need for a managed moves appeal process. If the parents do not wish to agree to a managed move they simply say so, without obligation. Of course, the school is then free to permanently exclude if they wish to.

DCSF regulations permit headteachers to convert a fixed-term exclusion to a permanent exclusion if additional information comes to light. The restorative conference invariably provides new information regarding the incident leading to it, and this gives grounds for the headteacher to come to a delayed decision.

At this point parents have the normal right of appeal against permanent exclusion. Neither parent nor pupil can be disadvantaged by being offered, or refusing, a managed move. Nor is the school disadvantaged. If they have good grounds for wanting the child to leave the school, and the parents refuse the managed move option, an appeal will be unsuccessful. If the school's grounds for wanting a managed move are flimsy, then it is only fair that parents have the opportunity to refuse it, and test whether the school will exclude, and whether any appeal will succeed.

Setting an example for other pupils

Sometimes headteachers want to take action in a way that sets an example to the rest of the school and the wider community. A managed move can achieve this objective as effectively as a permanent exclusion.

Example:
A pupil badly damaged a teacher's car before roaming the school shouting abuse and disturbing classes. He was not academic but loved sports. The headteacher was minded to permanently exclude him without a managed move option, as an example to others. The facilitator told the boy this at the home visit. The boy was able to express his remorse and said he hoped to go to a school specialising in sports. The headteacher of the sports school would only accept the pupil on a managed moves basis. The headteacher of his current school was persuaded to agree to this provided there was sufficient reparation. The damage was paid for, letters of apology were written to all the teachers affected, and the pupil agreed to apologise for his behaviour in front of the whole school.

The impact on the school culture and ethos

Once a school starts to use managed moves, staff and pupils will develop an interest in what this means. It could become just a euphemism for permanent exclusion.

It would be better if it is seen as an important warning, an event which can have positive outcomes, and a process in which pupils must take responsibility for their actions, be clear about what they really want and need, and generally act in an accountable, grown-up way.

A switch to managed moves changes the school culture for the better, and helps overcome staff demoralisation caused by the school exclusion ethos, which focuses on what pupils are doing wrong rather than what they are doing right.

Ideally, between a quarter and a half of managed move meetings will lead to a return to the same school. In this way, the gravity of the situation will be emphasised, and pupils will get the message:

> 'A managed move meeting means that you are probably going to have to leave the school. But if you *really* take responsibility for what you have done, and ask for and accept help, you might be lucky.'

So it is doubly important that headteachers call for a managed move meeting not only in cases where a situation has reached the end of the line, but in cases where it might be the end of the line, or where it is time to draw a line in the sand. One way to do this is to consider a deferred managed move agreement.

Deferred moves

A deferred move is a useful option. It is only actioned if the pupil does not keep their side of the agreement.

- The school agrees to provide a change in learning opportunities.
- Parents agree to support the plan, in every way they can.
- A contingency plan is agreed by all parties which identifies a move to a new setting if the first plan is unsuccessful in producing real change.

If the pupil is able to keep within agreed boundaries and successfully accesses the support they need then the pupil is able to stay in the school. If they do not, the next step is to let the parents know that a move is necessary, as agreed with them. However, the school must play its part in providing a change of opportunity.

Two paths to exclusion

There are two kinds of situation leading to permanent exclusion. One follows chronic problems, and the second arises because of a critical event. These require somewhat different responses.

A school may want to use the managed move process as a way of *avoiding* the need to permanently exclude a child. This could be because a fresh start has become possible, or because a temporary move to another setting followed by a return to the original school has become an option. Each case is unique, but the salient elements tend to follow a pattern.

Chronic problems

In a chronic situation, despite the best efforts of the school and other agencies over a period of time, the child is not thriving at school, the school community is being adversely affected and matters are coming to a head.

Typical issues include:
- Conflicts with peers across different school settings, such as class and playground.
- A running conflict with one or more teachers.
- Refusal to work.
- Behaviour that is persistently detrimental to the progress of other children and/or the child concerned.

There are three main early indicators that a chronic situation is reaching end-point:
- The pupil is taking an increasing and disproportionate amount of senior manager time.
- Teachers, other pupils, or other parents are complaining about the pupil and may also be taking unilateral action.
- Little is being achieved educationally for the pupil.

Example:
Alex is struggling to keep up with school work and often goes off task, chatting and distracting other pupils. When the teacher remonstrates, the situation frequently deteriorates into arguments and abuse, and Alex has taken to storming out of the classroom and disturbing other classes. Some teachers have started to refuse to have Alex in their lessons. Alex's attendance is also dropping alarmingly.

Typically, no one incident is sufficiently serious to warrant a permanent exclusion. However, the pressure of repeated incidents with their attendant time-cost leads to 'the slippery slope', and as the exclusion file gets bigger, and/or the number of fixed-term exclusion days handed out reaches the permitted limit, a moment of truth arrives.

Timing managed moves when there are chronic problems

It is best to initiate the managed move process at the beginning of the slippery slope, not at the end. Senior managers will then have time to make plans, talk with colleagues and arrange meetings. Crucially, the headteacher still has room to manoeuvre at this stage. For instance, the process may lead to a real change of heart for the pupil (and the parents and school) and a fresh start. The timing of the managed move conference also has a bearing on whether a deferred move is possible.

> Example:
> Nearly every week, the headteacher's time is taken up dealing with an incident involving Ronny and a teacher (usually a supply teacher) in a clash of wills followed by an argument. The most recent incident warrants a fixed-term exclusion and if repeated could lead to a permanent exclusion. The headteacher initiates the managed move process either with or just after the current fixed-term exclusion and does not wait for the final incident.

If the child is currently out of school on a fixed-term exclusion, it is best if the managed move meeting takes place before they return.

Critical events

When a serious event occurs in school, the whole community looks to the headteacher to act. Decisions need to be made quickly and feelings are often running very high. The headteacher is under pressure to respond and is not generally in a position to delay.

A single critical event can lead to the immediate permanent exclusion of a pupil with an otherwise spotless record.

Typical events include:
- Violence towards staff or pupils.
- Acts which endanger the safety of pupils and staff.
- Criminal offences.
- Flagrant breaches of school health, safety and behaviour codes.

> Example:
> A pupil brings a knife into school and threatens a teacher. When confronted the pupil runs out of school. Later he starts a fire in the school rubbish bins.

Timing managed moves when a critical event has occurred

The headteacher has the following options:
- Permanently exclude the child and then try to gain parental support for a managed move.
- Offer the pupil and parents a managed move meeting, after which a permanent exclusion or a managed move may take place.

The second option allows headteachers room to manoeuvre, and to gather more information before coming to a final decision.

Critical events are generally not foreseeable. However, the timing of any permanent exclusion can be. It is preferable to delay the final decision until the end of the managed move process for the following reasons:

- A far-reaching decision about permanent exclusion is better made when initial reactions have cooled.
- Even if the evidence seems overwhelming, it is only fair to consider possible contributory factors, and to give the wrong-doer a chance to put things right.

In a chronic situation, the managed move process and the permanent exclusions process can be kept separate. However, because a critical situation may well be a one-off event, the decisions can only be deferred within the time frame set down by the government for permanent exclusion. This is covered in more detail on pages 46–51.

Two model cases

A model managed move – chronic problems

Ruth, an attractive and volatile 14-year-old pupil, was unpopular with teachers, enjoyed confrontations, and was quick-witted enough to destabilise teachers, particularly younger males. She had few friends. Over the previous term her behaviour had become unpredictable and aggressive and she seemed impervious to sanctions. Before permanently excluding Ruth, the headteacher referred her to a voluntary agency facilitator working in partnership with the local authority.

The headteacher's referral: The headteacher was saddened by the situation but there was increasing pressure and he doubted Ruth would cope with public exams. He and the facilitator discussed alternative options. Appreciative enquiry by the facilitator revealed the headteacher's dilemma. The school could fund a college place which would be much better for Ruth. But if she did not succeed at college, the school would still have to pay for this place as well as for a Pupil Referral Unit (PRU) place. The headteacher trusted the facilitator enough to reveal that Ruth had 'got under his skin'. He could not explain her behaviour and viewed her as a destructive person with few redeeming features. He did not believe she would be any different at college.

The home visit: The facilitator spent two hours at the family home and met both parents with Ruth. This narrative emerged: her parents wanted to challenge any exclusion. Ruth's mother was a self-centred woman with her own unresolved issues who did not like her routines to be disrupted by Ruth being at home. Ruth did not get enough support and family discussions often ended with arguments, shouting and tears. Ruth played an adult role at home.

The facilitator was able to draw out a different character from Ruth. Despite appearances she was highly sensitive and responded to criticism with anger and hurt. She felt anxious about exams and hated being 'treated like a child'. She found school work difficult and did not get enough help in class. This made her anxious or angry and she would become disruptive and confrontational. She did not want to drop out, go to the PRU or stay at school. Her apparent lack of options added to the frustration.

In the safety of her own home and encouraged by the no-blame approach of the facilitator, Ruth was able to think about the effect she had on others. She was able to hear that the headteacher really was concerned and wanted to help her. She really liked the idea of going to college and was concerned by the headteacher's worries about this option. It was put to her that she could trust the headteacher, be willing to explain herself properly to him, apologise to teachers whom she had upset, and so demonstrate that she could act in a mature way. The facilitator thought this might persuade the headteacher to reconsider a college placement. Ruth was keen to do this, and her parents also agreed they would all benefit from some support and guidance to improve relationships at home. Ruth also needed some additional learning support.

After the home visit the facilitator had a long telephone discussion with the headteacher who said he was willing to consider the college option again if Ruth conducted herself appropriately at the conference.

The conference (family theme): Ruth and both parents met with the headteacher, a teacher representative and the facilitator in the local community hall (neutral territory). The conference script was followed (see pages 93–7) and, in the ensuing discussion, the headteacher was able to appreciate a different side to Ruth. She played her part and showed him that she could be responsible. She brought an employer's reference from the local teashop where she worked on Saturdays as proof that she could act responsibly if treated in an adult way.

Outcomes:

- The headteacher did not change his view that she could no longer stay in school, but he did decide that she would behave in college if given the chance.

- After seeing Ruth's reaction, her parents had decided that they would agree to the vocational course.
- Ruth's teachers were relieved by the outcome.
- Because it was a placement rather than an enrolment, Ruth actually stayed on roll at the school. In practice she did not go to the school again.
- She successfully completed the two-year college course.

A model managed move – critical event
At this school, the headteacher was determined to discourage drugs. During assembly, he laid down the law – any pupil in possession of drugs would be permanently excluded. The very next day John was challenged by a teacher to empty his pockets, and instead threw something to his friend Damian, who left the classroom with it. Later, a wrap of skunk was found in a rubbish bin. The teacher recognised the package, and John and Damian were questioned. John claimed the drugs belonged to Damian, who had 'planted' them on him as a joke. Damian denied this.

The headteacher's initial reaction was that both should be immediately and permanently excluded. However, he was reluctant to do so because the pupils were popular and of otherwise exemplary behaviour. Did he not have to follow through on his previous day's terrible warning at assembly? Staff were divided and the chair of governors was concerned about local press coverage.

The headteacher decided to consult the local managed moves agency, who had built up a reputation for safe handling of difficult situations. They saw the urgency and arranged an immediate visit to take the referral. The headteacher also agreed to inform the boys' parents of a 15 day fixed-term exclusion as an interim measure.

The headteacher's referral: The headteacher really appreciated having someone from outside the situation to help him think through his options, and also how to present the case so that staff, children and parents received the right messages. Whilst technically both pupils had been 'in possession' their roles were not identical and the headteacher wanted to reflect on this and gather more information before making a decision. The fixed-term exclusion gave him this time. The facilitator made sure that he had understood the headteacher's position correctly: at least one pupil would have to leave the school and he was minded to do this through permanent exclusion as an example to the school. However, if the headteacher could really get to the bottom of the situation, he might not have to exclude both.

The home visit: One of the facilitator's roles is to establish all-party consensus on what happened. Disputes of fact should be cleared up before the conference. In this case, the truth would have been hard to establish without home visits.

The narrative was similar at both houses. The parents were not drug-users and were shocked, not wanting to believe their child was in such trouble. The facilitator explained that if they could be supportive their son would find it easier to tell the truth. Both families were encouraged that a permanent exclusion could be avoided even if a change of school was not. They could also see that unless the boys told the same story, both would be permanently excluded. It took several explanations, but eventually the boys saw that the one who had brought the drugs into school could save his friend and make things better for himself by owning up. It turned out that Damian had brought the cannabis into school and that both boys were going to try it out after school that day. He had put the drugs in John's pocket on impulse 'as a joke'.

Both boys came to see that their future lay in their own hands. The school might offer them a solution, but they were going to have to take responsibility for their actions and to convince the headteacher that they were telling the truth about what happened.

The conference (justice theme): At the meeting both boys stated in plain terms what had happened and offered apologies. The headteacher agreed that John had been under pressure and would probably have been in just as much trouble if he had handed over the cannabis straight away. Damian's parents asked if he could have a managed move instead of a permanent exclusion. The headteacher was reluctant to allow this but did so on condition that Damian would agree to attend a drugs counselling session (Damian's suggestion), and the headteacher further requested that he write a letter for the school magazine explaining why he had to leave the school and how he felt about that. A new school had already been identified for Damian, and the Head of Year attended the conference and signed the agreement. John offered to apologise to the teacher concerned and to do community service at the school. The headteacher also asked him to apologise in assembly.

Outcomes:
- Damian went to a new school on a managed move and John stayed on.
- Both boys found their reparation tasks daunting.
- Damian's parents had made a commitment to ensure he kept his side of the bargain. His letter was short but surprisingly moving and it was published alongside his picture in the school magazine. The struggle to

get him to attend the counselling opened up some family issues and the family asked for group counselling some time later.

- John found it mortifying to stand in front of the school and to apologise to the staff and other pupils for a flagrant breach of the school code and for wasting staff time. Although he squirmed and blushed he actually did it quite well and several teachers came up later that day with a friendly word and some encouragement. He also spent 10 lunchtimes in the AVA room doing photocopying.
- Damian succeeded at his new school, and John kept himself out of serious trouble. There were no further drug incidents at the school.

Chapter 4

EXPLAINING MANAGED MOVES TO THE SCHOOL COMMUNITY

The information sheets provided here will be useful to schools and other agencies when it comes to explaining managed moves to different groups. This information can be adapted and reproduced as needed.

Information for pupils

The tone of this section may seem surprising. It is written as if the headteacher is talking to the pupils. Pupils will hear a very positive message about managed moves but also be clear that it is not a soft option.

MANAGED MOVES – PUPILS' GUIDE

All you need to know about managed moves
Managed moves are a new way to help young people who are not succeeding at school or who breach our school codes.

   All our teachers try their best to make sure every pupil is happy at this school and learns to the best of their ability. Sometimes, we do not succeed as well as we would like. Some pupils might need a fresh start or a different learning programme to the ones we are able to provide here.

   Sometimes, pupils are unhappy because the school is too far from home, or their friends are elsewhere, or there are difficulties outside school which make it hard for them to learn.

   We know that when people are unhappy they show it in different ways. Some show it by not succeeding. Some find themselves getting into conflict with other pupils or their teachers. Some get very withdrawn and shut everyone else out. Some break the school codes and get into trouble.

   If these difficulties become very serious, or if you do something seriously wrong, then the school might ask you to consider a managed move to a new school. This is a voluntary process, so you do not have to agree to it if you don't wish to. But if you do we will find it much easier to help you find a new school. If you have done something wrong we will ask you to do your best to put it right whether or not you leave the school.

Our school prefers not to exclude people but we will do so if we have to. If we do need to consider exclusion, you will usually be invited to a managed move meeting to discuss the options before a final decision is made.

Information for parents

This guide is for parents who are being invited to a managed move meeting. Schools wishing to inform all parents about the managed moves policy can send this together with the pupils' guide and a covering letter. Alternatively, the two guides can be combined into the letter.

MANAGED MOVE MEETING – PARENTS' GUIDE

Managed moves are a new way to deal with offending behaviour
- This is a voluntary process for finding a new place or programme for children in difficulties. This might include a move to a new school, college or other placement and a new learning programme.
- It can often be used instead of the exclusion process or, if necessary, alongside it.
- At a managed move meeting, aggrieved people and their supporters meet with pupils who have caused problems and their supporters to talk about how to make up for the harm done.
- The pupils are given a chance to take responsibility for what they have done and, if possible, to make amends.
- The meeting also considers how to make sure the same thing does not happen again.

How it works
- The meeting coordinator contacts everyone involved to tell them what will happen and what they can do about it.
- Everybody has a chance to say what they think and feel about what happened and what they would like to see happen now.
- Sometimes teachers or other professionals will say what they think, too.

- We will then decide what needs to happen after the meeting. Parents have a choice about whether to agree to this.
- Wrong-doers often agree to make up in some way for what they did.

Information for staff

Schools may find the following key points list useful when explaining what a managed move is all about.

MANAGED MOVE MEETING – A GUIDE FOR STAFF

Managed moves are a new way to deal with offending behaviour
- Managed moves are a new voluntary process for dealing with children whose behaviour is causing serious concern. It offers an opportunity to avoid permanent exclusion when it becomes necessary to arrange for pupils to move from one school to another, or to a different educational setting such as a Pupil Referral Unit, college or work placement.
- A managed move meeting, led by an impartial facilitator, will take place at which decisions relating to the future learning of the pupil will be agreed.
- Everyone affected by the events which triggered the meeting is invited to participate.
- The meeting will have a justice theme (for offending behaviour) or a family theme (for social and personal issues) and is often a mixture of both.
- Outcomes will include reconciliation and reparation for injured parties, agreement as to the best course of action, and genuine mutual goodwill.
- If the school is requesting a change of outlook and behaviour from the pupil, it also needs to ensure that they are offered a change of opportunity.
- Whilst participation in the managed move process is voluntary, agreements made are seen as binding.
- Managed moves are supported by professional communities, families and friends and the facilitator.
- Managed moves create an ideal context for healing and real change.
- Managed moves are not 'out of' or 'into' provision but are 'within' a community-based network of learning opportunities.
- The key question is 'How can we meet the whole learning needs of this child?'
- In order for the parents to agree a move they will need to know what their child is moving to. The facilitator must always explain to the parents that they have the option to refuse the offer.

- Even if a pupil is permanently excluded a managed move meeting may still be held to decide where the child will go next.

Information for governors

Governors should be provided with the information sheets for staff, parents and pupils. In addition they will need the following guidelines.

MANAGED MOVES – GOVERNORS' GUIDE

- Managed moves are a new voluntary process for dealing with children whose behaviour is causing serious concern. It offers an opportunity to avoid permanent exclusion when it becomes necessary to arrange the movement of pupils from one school to another, or to a different educational setting such as a Pupil Referral Unit, college or work placement.
- The managed move process will usually be initiated when a pupil is at risk of permanent exclusion.
- However, it can be used in the absence of any exclusions activity.
- In order to make the process as effective as possible in changing pupil behaviour and helping them make positive progress it may sometimes be advisable for the headteacher to:

  Give a pupil a fixed-term exclusion of 15 days which is later converted to a permanent exclusion.

  Give a pupil a permanent exclusion but revoke it before the disciplinary committee meeting.
- Both these actions are permitted by current government regulations.[19]
- If a fixed-term or permanent exclusion has been given, government guidelines will be followed in the normal way as regards governors' involvement.[20]
- A managed move meeting normally takes place 10 to 15 days after the parents are notified by letter.
- The disciplinary committee will therefore meet, if required, on the 14th or 15th day after the exclusion letter has been sent out.
- If the disciplinary committee does meet, it will act in the usual way to consider any exclusion or managed move.

19 http://www.teachernet.gov.uk/wholeschool/behaviour/exclusion/guidance/part3/, see paragraph 67 (last accessed August 2007).
20 http://www.teachernet.gov.uk/wholeschool/behaviour/exclusion/guidance/part4/, see paragraph 75ff (last accessed August 2007).

Chapter 5

THE MANAGED MOVE PROCESS FROM START TO FINISH

This chapter describes the main stages in the managed move process. From the schools' perspective this includes appointing and briefing the facilitator; informing the parents; the home visit; and the managed move meeting – how it works, and what follows on from it.

Appointing a facilitator

The first action is to contact whoever facilitates managed moves in your education community to arrange a referral meeting (see page 25).

The lack of a trained facilitator need not be a barrier. This book sets out a method for managed moves that is robust and effective. A member of staff with sufficient time and the required skills might be asked to carry it out, using Part 3 as a guide.

Letting the parents know

Parents must be kept properly informed of what is happening and advised of their rights. The headteacher will need to write to the parents explaining the circumstances surrounding the managed move meeting. This letter is likely to raise anxiety but it also conveys important implicit messages to the parent and child about what may happen next.

Because parents of children who get into trouble are more likely (than average) to have difficulties with reading, the letter sent to them should be short and clear. Government guidance on exclusion issued in 2006 recommends sending a letter nearly 500 words long – a length which could be daunting for many recipients. Sample letters for different situations can be found on pages 46–51.

The referral meeting

In this face-to-face meeting with the facilitator, the headteacher (or their delegate) sets out the basic case history, the current situation and what led up to it. The facilitator listens to the headteacher's narrative, and, as appropriate, the staff's, including a summary assessment of the child.

The facilitator seeks to understand the background to the story, and to flesh out the account, exploring the positive aspects of the child and the situation as well as the negative, and begins to get an understanding of the child's learning needs.

The next step is to explore the grey areas, the alternatives and the options. The headteacher needs to clarify how far they are willing to go, and under what conditions (if any) the child might return to the school.

Is it possible for this child to turn things around? What might the school do to provide a change of opportunity? Will the child agree to the plan and are they able to do what is required of them to justify their remaining on roll? A great deal may be demanded, including reparation, atonement, apologies, attendance for support work such as mentoring, and adherence to agreements on timetables, conduct and other special terms.

One of the facilitator's roles is to act as interlocutor, diplomat, and go-between on behalf of the headteacher. They need to truly and fairly hold the headteacher's view and be aware of how this should be shared with the parents in an appropriate way. At the home visit the parents and child will be in a position to think through the options frankly and informally and, with support, decide how to respond.

The facilitator needs therefore to be someone whom all parties can trust.

Involving providers of alternative placements and other professionals

In order for the parents to agree a move they will need to know what their child is moving *to*. The facilitator must find out what the education community can provide. The key person here may be another headteacher, or the head of the local authority inclusion team, Pupil Referral Unit (PRU) or local authority panel. Although resourcing issues can be problematic, the local authority is obliged to provide a full-time education programme for the child if they are permanently excluded.

Discussions may take place with other staff, other parents, psychologists, social workers, police or voluntary workers involved in the case or local authority representatives. The key questions are:

* What is *your* story?
* What is *your* assessment?
* How have you been affected by the situation?
* What would you like to see happen now?

The facilitator is also well-placed to carry out a comprehensive assessment for intervention, which can be done in collaboration with other agencies (see pages 53–4).

The home visit

The importance of the home visit cannot be overestimated. The facilitator goes to the home as a guide and support, not as a figure of authority. The home visit may be the first time that the parents and child have ever been truly 'heard' and given unconditional positive regard.

Many parents have stories to tell about their own unhappy schooldays. Listening to and involving them in resolving their child's difficulties at school can help break the cycle of social alienation which can afflict generations of families.

The parents and child will have formed their own narrative and assessment of the events which led to this visit. The parents frequently base their assessment on the child's, which can be partial in every sense of the word. The facilitator, who has already heard one or more versions of the story, helps the parents and child to revise and refine theirs. The facilitator can also guide the family to review the child's options and expectations and to develop a positive response.

The home visit is like a practice run for the conference. Parents and child can be supported to put their position and make their requests and offers clearly and positively. The facilitator also collects information about other family members whose support could be helpful. Facilitators frequently gather valuable information and insights that are new to the school and the education community during the home visit.

The facilitator needs to know the education system thoroughly and be satisfied that the options on offer to the child are fair. Facilitators should always explain to the parents and child that they have the option to refuse the offer, even if this means the child may be permanently excluded, and that in this case the parents would be able to appeal. They should not collude with the headteacher or the parents.

The managed move meeting (the restorative conference)

The conference should involve everyone who has been affected by the situation, and everyone who would be affected by its outcome.

This includes:

- At least one school representative (ideally the headteacher).
- The child and their family, including friends or supporters.
- Any members of the school community who have been harmed by the pupil's behaviour (or someone who can represent their views) and their supporters.
- One or more people who will be responsible for the ongoing plan (if available).

The numbers tend to range from four (plus facilitator) to ten. If any parties do not attend, the facilitator may be able to bring their views to the meeting – although this is not ideal.

Participants are usually tense and anxious at first, and there may be moments of drama and high emotion, so the facilitator needs to be skilled in interpersonal and group work.

It is important to recognise the reciprocal roles of the child and family and the education community. **If a pupil is being requested to change their outlook and behaviour, they need to be offered a change of opportunity.**

If the steps set out in this guide are followed the outcome will be:

- Reconciliation and reparation for injured parties.
- A sense that the situation has been resolved as well as could be.
- A sense of unity of purpose and genuine mutual goodwill.
- An agreement which all parties are content to sign. It is both good psychology and in keeping with the voluntary ethic to ask the child to sign as well.

The managed move agreement

- A managed move agreement is parent- and pupil-friendly.
- Although made voluntarily, all parties should treat the agreement as binding. It should be used alongside, and inform, any formal planning documentation.
- It should be drafted in the simplest possible language and kept short: a typical agreement consists of between five and ten sentences.
- It should outline the key points of the move, such as when, where and what will happen next, and the form in which this needs to be set down for educational purposes – usually a new or modified individual education plan (IEP).
- It should identify the person tasked with working across the community to ensure the move is implemented.
- It may include terms requested by representatives of the original or future setting, or by the parents and child.
- It should explicitly outline any change of outlook on the part of the parents and child, and the change of opportunity provided for the child.
- Incentives and goals should be described in terms of achievement (e.g. completed learning or therapeutic activities) rather than behaviour.

A sample agreement:
- Hamed has apologised to the pupil he attacked and promised not to bear any grudges towards him. His apology was accepted.
- Hamed agrees to attend the PRU for the rest of this school year and concentrate on improving his English and Maths skills.
- Hamed's parents agree that he should transfer to the PRU as soon as possible.
- The Head of the PRU, John Naismith, will support Hamed's move.
- Hamed will also take part in a programme provided by the youth group LiftOff to help him understand and manage his frustration.
- The school will allow Hamed to continue with after-school archery training, which is not available at the PRU, provided he continues to participate positively in this and does not come to the school at any other times.
- At the end of this school year, if Hamed has made good progress and wishes to return to mainstream education the PRU will help him find a place.
- At the moment, this school does not wish to consider his return. However, depending on reports received about his progress, the headteacher may be willing to consider this in the future.

Managed moves at a glance

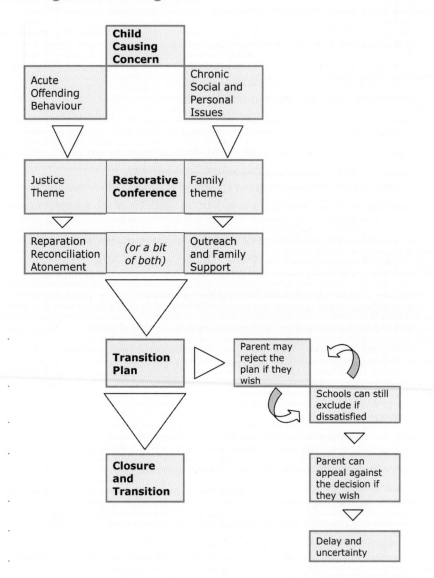

While a child may present chronic personal and social issues for a long period of time there comes a point where matters come to a head. The managed move process should then follow a similar time frame to the process for acute situations. The conference often considers wider issues in the light of the final incident, which in itself may not be serious.

Who does what when a managed move takes place?

The headteacher (or their delegate)
- Acts on concerns over a pupil arising from a chronic or acute situation.
- Sends the appropriate letter to the parents.
- Contacts whoever facilitates managed moves in their area.
- Arranges a referral meeting with the facilitator.

The facilitator
- Receives the referral from the headteacher.
- Confirms the headteacher's voluntary participation.
- Begins to compile a participant list (those affected by the situation and those who will be affected by or involved with the managed move).
- Collects contact information.
- Agrees a provisional timetable and neutral venue for the conference.
- Helps the headteacher to form a provisional transition plan and reviews the options and choices.
- Agrees with the headteacher who will contact the receiving agency or agencies and how.
- Arranges home visits.
- Contacts other participants.
- Contacts potential receiving agencies, if agreed.
- Guides all participants and agencies through the conference process.
- Liaises with the headteacher.
- Sends invite letters.

The child and family
- Tell their story.
- Confirm their voluntary participation.
- Take advice as necessary.
- Review the provisional transition plan.
- Consider their options and choices.

Other participants
- Tell their story.
- Confirm their voluntary participation.

Receiving agencies
- Agree their part in the provisional transition plan.
- Confirm their voluntary participation.

At the conference all participants listen to each other and seek the following objectives:

- Reparation, reconciliation and atonement (as necessary).
- Recognition of the child's needs and agreement of a transition plan that will meet them.
- Delegation of responsibilities going forward.
- A clear statement of what the child, family, schools and education agencies will do.
- Closure and transition.

Timeline for involving families and governors

Day 1	Day 2	Day 3–5	Days 6–10	By Day 14	Day 15
Exclusions letter[21]	Managed move letter	Schools referral meeting	Facilitator activity	Managed move meeting	Disciplinary committee meeting[22]

This timeline ensures that the school meets its statutory requirements without impeding the managed move process. If the headteacher wants to send only one letter to the family it goes out on Day 1.

Sample letters for five different situations

When writing to the family a delicate balance between mandatory and voluntary approaches must be maintained. The headteacher should be aware of the potential difference between what he writes and what the parents and child may read into it. The 'message' that the letter sends to the family is as important as the content, acting as a lever for a more constructive response. Will the letter motivate the pupil and parents to act positively?

---

21 Usually a 15 day fixed-term exclusion letter (although a managed move can also be preceded by a permanent exclusion).

22 This must be held by the 15th day if there is a permanent exclusion or a 6–15 day fixed-term exclusion and the parents request it. If the permanent exclusion is withdrawn the meeting does not need to take place (unless the parents request it).

23 http://www.teachernet.gov.uk/wholeschool/behaviour/exclusion/guidance/part3/modelletter2/ (last accessed August 2007).

When the managed move process has been initiated in the absence of any exclusions procedure

Comment	There are good grounds for believing the child really would benefit from a change of school. This is an opportunity for the parents to address grave concerns without blame and with help.
SAMPLE A	Dear [name of parent] I have been concerned for some time now about the progress [pupil name] is making and whether this school is the best place for him to be educated. *Insert details as appropriate of recent causes for concern expressed in matter-of-fact language. Statements of fact always sound more reasonable than judgements and evaluative statements.* It would be very helpful if you would come to a meeting to discuss my concerns. I have asked [name of facilitator], who will arrange the meeting, to get in touch with you in the next few days. They will explain what will happen at the meeting.
Leverage for change	The opportunity to put things right before a permanent exclusion becomes inevitable.
Message	'Work with the school and services and we can resolve this situation amicably.'

When the headteacher has given the pupil a fixed-term exclusion, as a cooling-off period or for the school to consider what outside agencies might contribute to stabilising the situation

Comment	A headteacher in this position is genuinely asking parents to consider an alternative but has already made the decision that this incident is not 'the final straw'.
SAMPLE B	Send DCSF regulation model letter 2[23] with the following paragraph added:

It would be very helpful if you would come to a meeting to discuss this exclusion. I have asked [name of facilitator], who will arrange the meeting, to get in touch with you in the next few days. They will explain what will happen at the meeting.

OR

Send DCSF regulation model letter 2 and this short letter the next day:

Dear [name of parent]
I wrote to you yesterday to inform you of my decision to exclude [pupil name]. Although the information provided in that letter still applies it would be very helpful if you would come to a meeting to discuss this exclusion. I have asked [name of facilitator], who will arrange the meeting, to get in touch with you in the next few days. They will explain what will happen at the meeting.

Leverage for change	The opportunity to put things right before a permanent exclusion becomes inevitable.
Message	'Work with the school and services and we can resolve this situation amicably.'

Where the situation is more serious and it *is* the final straw or a critical incident has occurred that could warrant permanent exclusion but the headteacher would like time to reflect

Comment	An immediate decision seems to be needed and the next 15 days are critical. Paragraph 67 of current DCSF regulations makes clear that the headteacher has several options.[24] In this case the head gives a fixed-term exclusion pending further evidence being gathered. This is quite legitimate because the managed move process will certainly reveal new information.

24 'In exceptional cases — usually where further evidence has come to light — a fixed period exclusion may be extended, or converted to a permanent exclusion. In such cases the headteacher must write again to the parents explaining the reasons for the change.' http://www.teachernet.gov.uk/wholeschool/behaviour/exclusion/guidance/part3/, see paragraph 67 (last accessed August 2007).

> The facilitator should be clear whether a return to school is also a possibility. The headteacher may be genuinely undecided or be primarily offering the pupil a more positive way out.

SAMPLE C	Use either version of sample letter B adding optionally the following paragraph:
	You need to know that I am still gathering further information about this situation, after which I may make this exclusion permanent.

Leverage for change	The threat of permanent exclusion combined with the possibility of avoiding it are both powerful incentives for the child and parents to try to meet the headteacher's needs for the school community's well-being. Some finesse is called for here: the headteacher writes formally to the parents, and the facilitator talks informally about 'what can be achieved' at the home visit.

Message	'It's not permanent yet but unless you convince me otherwise, it could/will be.'

When the headteacher has made up his mind to pursue a permanent exclusion but might withdraw it under certain specific conditions

Comment	This situation will motivate the pupil the most but may also raise anxieties and counter-productive thoughts and feelings. The headteacher must inform the parents by letter that the pupil has been given a permanent exclusion while indicating that powers to withdraw the permanent exclusion do exist and it might be possible to do so at the managed move meeting.[25] This is most applicable when there is a specific issue which could be resolved (whether this is likely or not) and the head *will* withdraw the exclusion if the pupil takes responsibility for the issue and demonstrably deals with it.

25 'The headteacher may withdraw an exclusion that has not yet been reviewed by the governing body.'
Note that 'governing body' includes 'disciplinary committee' if there is one.
http://www.teachernet.gov.uk/wholeschool/behaviour/exclusion/guidance/part3/, see paragraph 67
(last accessed August 2007).

SAMPLE D   Send DCSF regulation model letter 4[26] with the following paragraph added:

It would be very helpful if you would come to a meeting to discuss this exclusion. I have asked [name of facilitator], who will arrange the meeting, to get in touch with you in the next few days. They will explain what will happen at the meeting.

Although the exclusion is permanent, it is within my power to withdraw it. However, I am unlikely to do so unless the issues raised in this letter are addressed by the time of meeting.

OR

Send DCSF regulation model letter 4 and this short letter the next day:

Dear [name of parent]

I wrote to you yesterday to inform you of my decision to exclude [pupil name]. Although the information provided in that letter still applies it would be very helpful if you would come to a meeting to discuss this exclusion. I have asked [name of facilitator], who will arrange the meeting, to get in touch with you in the next few days. They will explain what will happen at the meeting.

Although the exclusion is permanent, it is within my power to withdraw it. However, I am unlikely to do so unless the issues raised in my letter dated [previous day's date] are addressed by the time of meeting.

Leverage for change	The threat of permanent exclusion is strong and the possibility of avoiding it is weak. Although this creates the maximum pressure to change it can also act as a disincentive, especially if the child feels alienated. However, if there are *specific* things the pupil could do to resolve the situation then the pupil can make positive choices.
Message	'It is permanent unless you convince me otherwise. If you can't or won't resolve the situation then a move is the best option.'

26 http://www.teachernet.gov.uk/wholeschool/behaviour/exclusion/guidance/part3/modelletter4/ (last accessed August 2007).

When the headteacher has made up his mind to pursue a permanent exclusion without alternatives

Comment	In this situation the objective is to help the child move on to a more effective educational setting following permanent exclusion. The risk of alienation and rejection is high.
SAMPLE E	Send DCSF regulation model letter 4[27] with the following paragraph added:
	It would be very helpful if you would come to a meeting to discuss this exclusion. I have asked [name of facilitator], who will arrange the meeting, to get in touch with you in the next few days. They will explain what will happen at the meeting.
	OR
	Send DCSF regulation model letter 4 and this short letter the next day:
	Dear [name of parent] I wrote to you yesterday to inform you of my decision to exclude [pupil name]. Although the information provided in that letter still applies it would be very helpful if you would come to a meeting to discuss this exclusion. I have asked [name of facilitator], who will arrange the meeting, to get in touch with you in the next few days. They will explain what will happen at the meeting.
Leverage for change	Following permanent exclusion a move still has to take place and this will be achieved more positively if all parties meet to discuss how the pupil's needs can best be met. A successful managed move meeting reduces the likelihood that parents will appeal against the decision.
Message	'You are permanently excluded but we want you to continue your education elsewhere and have a chance to succeed like everyone else.'

---

27 http://www.teachernet.gov.uk/wholeschool/behaviour/exclusion/guidance/part3/modelletter4/ (last accessed August 2007).

Chapter 6

MOVING ON – WHAT ARE THE OPTIONS?

The alternative learning offer

In this guide, the term 'alternative learning offer' is used to describe the learning programme (outlined in the managed move agreement) which the facilitator, the current school, and the alternative education provider will develop in response to their assessment of the needs of the pupil and family. It is the hardest part of the managed move to get right.

The alternative learning offer needs to identify the learning programme, where it will take place (the setting), and any plans for further moves or developments, depending on progress. The facilitator will have discussed with the parents how well this offer meets the pupil's needs. In an ideal world the quality of the offer would determine whether parents decide to accept it. In reality, the options will be limited by what the locality can provide.

Although it is important for a child to have a broad and balanced curriculum over the course of their whole education, there are times when an individual might benefit from provision that focuses mainly on personal and social development. This is especially true of children who need a managed move. Some children are not ready to participate in a highly structured framework of study and examination. For them, commitment to a conventional full-time education should be replaced by a commitment to meeting their broader needs, realism about what can be achieved, and an aspiration to engage the child in supported learning after they have left school.

A pivotal change in thinking is necessary: instead of trying to develop individual education plans (IEPs) that look like school, or clinging to the principles of the National Curriculum, we should develop an approach to education planning that meets the needs of the whole child and which is not necessarily limited to national minimum standards.

The alternative learning offer must be based on a comprehensive assessment of the pupil and should:

- Make a step change in the learning offer. This can mean moving to another school, college or Pupil Referral Unit (PRU), or an individualised programme based around home learning. It could also mean a fresh start at the original school or deferred return to it with an IEP which identifies new, more appropriate opportunities for learning.

- Consider all the child's needs — personal and social learning, learning for life, and academic study.
- Offer choices for the child — for instance an option to return to mainstream education after a period in a specialist setting.
- Draw on the resources of the whole community to provide additional education settings, for example, family learning, community-based options, voluntary agency support and/or specialist input could be combined with part-time learning in a mainstream school or other setting.

Comprehensive assessment

The Every Child Matters Common Assessment Framework (CAF) should be used whenever appropriate to help draw up the assessment.[28] The highest priority is to help children and families to develop positive motivation, identify and achieve realistic goals, and then move on to new ones.

The facilitator should rely on and collaborate with other agencies involved, such as mental health services, to achieve a fair and pertinent analysis. The following key points should be covered.

The assessment should identify:
- What needs are not being met.
- Why this is so.
- What the child's immediate life goals are.
- How the agencies involved can help in achieving these goals.
- How the family/carers can support this.
- How the unmet needs can be met.
- What can be done to remove or reduce inhibiting factors.
- What can be done to accelerate learning and development.
- Motivational levers for child and family members.
- The critical pathway to success and key milestones.

Areas covered by the assessment should include:
- Case background.
- Family relationships and dynamics.

---

28 'The Common Assessment Framework (CAF) is a key part of delivering frontline services that are integrated and focused around the needs of children and young people. The CAF is a standardised approach to conducting an assessment of a child's additional needs and deciding how those needs should be met. It can be used by practitioners across children's services in England.' http://www.everychildmatters.gov.uk/deliveringservices/caf/ (last accessed August 2007).

- Hidden needs.
- School curriculum learning needs.
- Personal and social learning needs especially to do with relationships.
- Child and family strengths and weaknesses.
- Motivational opportunities and inhibitors, and obstacles to progress.
- Additional support needs.

Who is responsible for arranging the alternative learning setting?

The alternative learning setting may be identified by the headteacher of the initial school, or by the facilitator. However, it is likely that the first approach to the setting in question will come from the local authority. There are no fixed rules.

In localities where there is a managed move team, the school may receive a good deal of help in identifying possible placements. In other areas it will be up to the headteacher.

If the pupil's needs are best served by a move to alternative education, then the school will refer the child to the local authority, which will have channels for managing children coming out of mainstream schooling, such as an inclusion management team or the special needs department. Agencies such as education welfare or psychology services may provide case officers. If the move is from mainstream to mainstream the school might make the first suggestion and contact.

Exploring the possibilities

Most managed moves will fall into one of these categories:

- Reconciliation and an immediate fresh start at the current school.
- Transfer to another school or college, probably with additional therapeutic input, and possibly with an adjusted learning programme.
- Part-time attendance at the current school with an individual learning and therapeutic programme off-site, for a fixed period, followed by review.
- Full-time attendance at the PRU followed by a return to the current school or by entry into a new school or college.
- Part-time attendance at the PRU combined with a home and community learning plan.
- A programme (which may be based around home learning) which is individually tailored to a child's special requirements, usually for children with considerable needs.

Age-appropriate planning

It is important to consider the child's age in deciding between the possible options. Generally, the younger the child the more likely it is that the plan will need to specify short-term and long-term objectives and options. Children over 14 who are in their public exam years are more likely to be moving on to a final placement which may include college and work experience. Exclusion rates rise at secondary school and peak at around the age of 13. For this group, a managed move should usually specify a mainstream setting in the long term, if not the short term.

Staying in the mainstream

If the most crucial issues can be addressed quickly then the solution is more likely to be another mainstream school. However, if they take time to address then there are stronger grounds for considering an alternative placement.

Transition back to the mainstream can be triggered by the achievement of 'threshold criteria', which should be outlined in the agreement where possible. For instance, completing an anger management programme and writing an article on 'How I learned to manage my feelings' could be two 'threshold criteria' (among others) that enable a return to school, or entrance to a new mainstream school.

The headteacher and staff of a mainstream school are likely to be more willing to accept a pupil through a managed move if the evidence of unmet needs is clearly spelled out together with an explanation as to:

- What has been done to meet these needs already.
- What will be done by outside agencies to further meet these needs.
- What additional resources the community will bring into the school to address any further outstanding needs.

The receiving headteacher will be more hopeful and reassured if (in some shape or form) a clear statement by the pupil is given (verbally or in writing) describing:

- Their understanding of why they have had to leave their initial school.
- How their outlook has changed during the managed move period.
- Why they believe they can be successful in a new setting.
- How their behaviour will be different.
- What help they would like in order to make a success of their new placement.

Dual placement

Under dual placement a child can be educated in a new school or other educational setting while remaining on the roll of the current school. If the new placement fails, a voluntary agreement can ensure that the initial school still has legal responsibility. This can facilitate the managed move process by helping parents to be realistic about the options and reassuring the new school that it won't be 'stuck with the problem'. If the placement does fail, usually the student returns to the original school. Often their attitude has changed as a result of the managed move and, if the school is willing to try again, a return can be surprisingly effective.

However, in some cases a return may trigger another crisis leading to permanent exclusion. The current school may also permanently exclude a pupil whose placement elsewhere has failed if it was made clear to the family when the placement was first agreed that this would happen if the placement went wrong. Needless to say dual placement works much better when the current school is prepared to have the pupil back.

Non-school programmes

A child who has an individualised programme needs to be enrolled somewhere. Typically, they can be enrolled at the nearest PRU, even if they are seldom or never on site.

The parameters of personal and social learning

Personal and social learning can be based on such themes as developing emotional intelligence, managing anger or understanding friendship.

Personal and social learning programmes will be more effective if they tackle aspects of a young person's life that are likely to encourage antisocial activity, such as a network of friends involved in delinquency or poor parental supervision.

The most effective methods for engaging young people in learning new skills or changing thinking patterns or attitudes associated with antisocial behaviour are:

- Interpersonal skills training – helping young people to interact effectively with others.
- Behavioural interventions such as role-playing.
- Cognitive skills training to address counter-productive thoughts and behaviours.
- Mentoring linked to individual counselling.
- Structured individual counselling (e.g. with a problem-solving framework).
- Specially trained staff acting in a parental role.[29]

'Behaviour modification' only works if the pupil is motivated to change. Simplistic reward and punishment formulas do not work, though incentives for achievement (not behaviour) and clear boundaries are both important.

How to involve families in the learning process

Parents constitute the largest unused community resource. Not every family can help, but many can. Family learning projects draw parents into a supported and supportive role in their child's progress in school and enable schools to use teacher-managed home learning as part of an alternative programme.

Family support can be highly flexible, reducing demand on resources as well as the need for managed transfer to special settings. A spin-off is that a small team of parent learning mentors may be developed over time, who can help other parents and even work in school as learning supporters. Family learning can also provide a context for therapeutic work.

During family learning sessions, specialist teachers model good teaching/parenting, which parents can emulate. Teachers can also observe parent/child interactions and moderate them. Pupils, meanwhile, can observe appropriate adult-to-adult interactions and emulate them. All parties can share and address crucial child develop-

---

29 *Offending Behaviour Programmes, Key Elements of Effective Practice*, edn 1 (London, Youth Justice Board, 2002), p. 9, Service Delivery.

ment issues. Parents are taught basic teaching skills. Pupils and parents are given homework, which the teacher evaluates, and any difficulties are discussed together.

Family learning projects are not hard to set up. Parents get the idea quickly and can adapt to the new activities at home. Once a family learning project is established, the positive relationships which have been developed are there as a flexible resource. For instance, if there are problems in school, more immediate feedback can reach the family and their response is likely to be more accommodating, collaborative and effective.

What is a 'learning activity'?

The case study given on page 60 provides an unusual example of what an aptitude-appropriate activity might be. However, individually tailored options could include attendance at a school specialising in vocational studies, or an opportunity to do more work-based learning.

In an attempt to give a clear framework to non-traditional activities that a young person might find valuable for learning, the following criteria may be useful:

- An alternative learning activity is always managed by a qualified teacher. About five hours of learning can be achieved with one hour of supervision by a teacher.
- Learning activities are planned activities based on current assessed ability or development, and relate to the child's IEP.
- The child's role is clear.
- The activity is safely supervised by a responsible adult whose role is clear.
- All relevant parameters are specified (for instance where, when and how the activity will take place, how long it will take, what resources are required and where they will be obtained, and when the activity review will take place).
- Intended outcomes are specifically itemised.
- Completed activities are followed by evaluation, two-way feedback and forward planning.

Any activity that conforms to these criteria could be used to help meet a child's IEP. The plan would set identifiable one-off learning goals rather than a more strategic timetabled approach which the children concerned might find hard to maintain.

Case studies

Reconciliation and an immediate fresh start in the current school
A pupil at a London school was constantly getting into conflicts with staff which often resulted in teachers becoming upset and angry. Staff were some-times too heavy-handed in response. The girl was also accused of bullying. The headteacher was on the brink of permanently excluding. A special mini restorative conference was arranged as a last-ditch attempt to resolve the

difficulties, with only the headteacher, the pupil and the facilitator. The head talked frankly about the situation and showed the pupil the letters of complaint received from parents and staff. The pupil explained her own grievances against teachers and the issues were fairly considered. The situation was resolved for quite some time; when it deteriorated again the headteacher was able to re-establish 'conference boundaries' and work with the pupil without further need of a facilitator. This led to a reduction in problems and the pupil did not have to move to another setting.

Transfer to another school

A pupil had been permanently excluded when he was 13 because of his attitudes to girls. He was frankly mad about them, and not at all bad looking. He could also be funny, impetuous, irresponsible and outrageous. This was an incendiary combination which frequently caused trouble. For instance, girls complained that he was looking at them in a strange way and one said that he had 'breathed on her neck in the dinner queue'. The final straw came when he chased a group of girls into the girls' toilets. His protestations that they had chased him into the boys' toilets fell on deaf ears.

At a managed move meeting the educational psychologist suggested a move to a boys school. The move went through quickly. He needed no support and succeeded very well, rapidly earning a place in the school football team. He freely admitted that the move had been a good thing because the absence of girls meant he could concentrate on his work.

There are clearly a number of equality and gender issues wrapped up in this story. Should more effort have been made to address his attitudes to girls? The psychologist judged that the issue was one of immaturity rather than deviancy and did not require intervention.

Transfer to another school, with additional therapeutic input

A pupil who repeatedly got into difficulties at school was invited to a restorative conference to discuss whether he could explain his behaviour and reassure the community that he appreciated the need for every member of it to be safe. The situation involved a boy-girl romance that had gone wrong. His behaviour was obsessive and he had pestered and distressed the girl's family and become threatening in his frustration. However, she was to some extent responsible. A great deal of light was thrown on the situation at the managed move conference. Although the girl agreed that she had blown hot and cold over the relationship, it was made clear to the boy that it was his behaviour that had breached safe and acceptable boundaries.

An agreement for a return to school was negotiated, along with a standing agreement that his parents would consent to a transfer to a school some distance away if the situation did not resolve. The same pattern re-emerged within a few weeks, and the pupil moved to the alternative school shortly afterwards. The receiving school had been represented at the conference and was able to provide appropriate support, especially guidance on maintaining balanced relationships.

Part-time attendance at school with home learning

A 14-year-old boy started to truant and often walked out of classes. He liked to spend time with the school-keeper and would help him with grass-cutting and other maintenance work. The headteacher preferred him to be on-site doing something useful rather than excluding him to roam around the town and get into trouble. At the home visit the facilitator discovered that, whilst his mother was alcoholic and could offer no help to the boy and his father was away on business for long hours every day, both his sisters could drive, had small children and were unemployed. At the managed move meeting it was agreed that he would have a part-time school programme combined with home learning.

His sisters took it in turns to bring him to school, exhort him to work and pick him up afterwards, and also helped with home learning. They were given training and advice and were paid car mileage expenses. They achieved good results quickly. For instance, within one week the boy could tell the time – something which he had shamefacedly admitted at the home visit he could not do.

Full-time attendance at a PRU followed by a return to the current school

A Year 10 pupil who worried about his mother's safety (because of her health) often feigned stomach-aches to get home. When the school put a stop to this, he made sure he got one-day exclusions instead. He felt isolated in school and lacked social skills, and teachers found him stubborn and rude. With the encouragement of a Connexions adviser, a managed move conference was arranged and he transferred to the PRU for a term.

A key worker there was able to win his trust and draw out his story. Arrangements were made for him to contact his mother whenever he needed. Through role play, the key worker was able to show the boy how his responses escalated problems with teachers, and to teach him some core social skills. Through creative visualisation, he was able to reduce his anxiety about being in a class. A 'week on a farm' break was arranged for him, and on the first night the farmer's wife discovered he was afraid of the dark. With her caring yet down-to-earth help, he gained a little self-confidence.

When he returned to school, arrangements were made for him to reassure himself that his mother was all right. He still found it very difficult to cope and often felt anxious about class activities and the possibility that he might be bullied. However, his week away had given him just enough courage to confront his fears. Once he was able to do this, his behaviour became much better and he went on to take the full complement of GCSEs.

An individually tailored programme

Jodie was 13 and hated school. Her lorry-driver father appeared to condone her truancy. When pressure was brought to bear the father always made sure she attended, and Jodie always made sure she got another exclusion. She would then join her father on his cross-country delivery runs.

During a restorative meeting someone thought to ask Jodie what she did like to learn about. She described her fascination with life on the road and with different types of heavy vehicle. She fully intended to become a lorry driver. She knew a great deal about lorries, such as how many wheels each type had. When encouraged to speak his mind, her father made it clear he really wanted her to be educated and would support any necessary steps, but hated to see her come home with another exclusion letter.

The meeting decided to see whether Jodie could keep to a part-time travelling learning programme which she would complete in her father's lorry cab. A programme of mathematics and geography activities was devised for her to do en route with her father's help. The maths and geography teachers went out of their way to track down suitable materials and soon had enough to keep her occupied. For instance, working out the distance travelled from the previous town every time they passed a road sign giving mileage helped her practice subtraction, and working out how many gallons of diesel they would need at the next stop, division. I-spy games were used to identify land features, and map-reading was also developed.

Her father proved to be excellent at mental arithmetic and was able to help her as he drove and to think of supplementary questions. They both loved it, and so did her maths and geography teachers. But the other teachers benefited, too, from a much more cooperative pupil who felt her needs and wishes were being heard. Although the quantity of learning was not great, the programme helped to maintain her connection with school and learning through a difficult time. And as soon as she reached Year 10 she was able to join the 'motor project' (a community-based project to develop car mechanic skills with free motocross sessions) and a college foundation course, having proved that if the community cooperated with her, she would cooperate in return – an important social learning experience for both parties.

Chapter 7

ADVICE FOR RECEIVING SCHOOLS

It is easier to start a new pupil at the beginning of a new term and easier still to do so at the beginning of a new year. It can be tough for any young person to make their way in a new school when all the other pupils seem to know each other. It is even harder if you come out of difficult circumstances and a turbulent school experience.

However, if the pupil can overcome the fear of change there are opportunities to meet new people and make new friends, and the chance to begin again with a fresh record and to revise 'How I see myself' and 'How I want others to see me.' The pupil can rely on being new to ask for help and discover how to approach things differently, with a fresh outlook and general goodwill. The child is most likely to succeed if they are able to feel a sense of belonging and of motivation.

The real tests of a managed move are its sustainability and its ability to deliver progress in learning. Should the move take place straightaway, or is it wise to allow a few weeks between the two schools, even if the move is from mainstream to mainstream? The answer depends on whether in the intervening time proactive steps can be taken to prepare the child for learning and for the challenge of a new environment. Some children benefit from a time to reflect and, frankly, to mourn their loss. However, those with a tendency to truant may find it harder to go back after even quite a short break. If specialist intervention is needed to address personal and developmental blocks to learning, it may be more effective before a return to school.

The induction meeting

Induction should be planned carefully, and an induction meeting held with the family before the child moves to the new school. The meeting should be attended by the headteacher of the new school (or designate), the class tutor, the child and parents, and the professional who took responsibility for supporting the transition at the managed move meeting.

The induction meeting is likely to take place after the managed move has been agreed in principle. Although the meeting should be supportive and child-focused, pertinent and sensitive questions need to be answered to the headteacher's satisfaction. These can be thought of as threshold criteria. It might even be useful for the future headteacher to keep these questions in mind and ask them, if appropriate, at the managed move meeting.

Before the meeting:
- The child and parents should have read the school rules, any home-school contract, and agreed to uphold them.
- They should have received a copy of the school's prospectus and, if possible, some information about the school's recent history.
- A 'written contract' for the pupil should be avoided at this stage if possible. It is not a morale-booster. The terms of any agreements made should be set at the managed move meeting.

At the meeting the future headteacher should:
- **Recognise** that there may be concerns, anxieties and (let's face it) fears on both sides.
- Tell the child and parents what the school's anxieties, concerns and fears are.
- Ask them to share theirs.
- Be reassuring – and describe the concrete steps the school can take to address their concerns.
- **Ask** the child how they see themselves.
- Headteachers might try using a SWOT analysis with the child – strengths, weaknesses, opportunities, threats.
- Headteachers should ask, 'What do you hope to achieve, what are your hopes, aspirations, and goals?'
- They should also ask 'How do you want others to see you?'
- **Show** the child a blank sheet of paper and say 'We want to start you with a clean sheet – a fresh record. But what should we tell the other pupils in your class about where you have come from?' This issue is at the heart of the matter. It is a tough question and may invoke strong emotions.
- A useful suggestion is 'Why don't you just tell your story to the class tutor?' This gives the pupil something to talk about with the tutor, and it gives the tutor a chance to hear first-hand about the past, and to explore the child's concerns and expectations.
- The headteacher and class tutor should help the child be clear about what they need to say to the class and how things should be presented.
- If appropriate, the tutor can join the headteacher in describing the new pupil to other staff, probably at a staff meeting.

After the induction meeting
The future headteacher will still need to answer the pupil's 'hidden' question: 'Who will meet my needs?'

- The headteacher should do what they can to make connections for the pupil within the school.
- The class tutor should 'champion' their new pupil, regularly checking how they are coping, and developing a relationship with them.
- It's hard to help a young person make friends. The best way is through involvement in extracurricular activities – for instance football or drama.
- Teachers can find roles for the child in school life – something simple, like taking the register back to the school office (with a 'friend' to show them the way).

Entry to the new school

Nothing is familiar – if possible and if appropriate the school should try to make the child's school entry gradual and easy.

- The headteacher would find it difficult to back-track on the agreement to accept the child, but a full-time start might be delayed for a few days if the headteacher is dissatisfied with the pupil's responses and attitude at the induction meeting. Any concerns should be raised in a frank but accommodating way. A pupil who is keen to join the school will usually respond positively at this point.
- Arrange for meetings with the pupil and their familiarisation with the site to take place when other pupils are not there and if appropriate over a week or two.
- If the move is being planned well in advance, a visit at the end of the previous term is advantageous.
- The child could have a trial one-hour lesson in the library or ICT resources centre.
- Ideally, the child should know the school site and environs, where to get lunch, and be made aware of any customs and practices that are idiosyncratic to the school.
- During the induction period the future headteacher should also make sure the pupil knows how to ask for help if they get into difficulties and where they can go if they want a safe place or assistance from their tutor.

Briefing staff

When explaining the situation to staff, the headteacher should be as positive as possible, and give them some idea of what difficulties or disadvantages this child may have or have had. It is not appropriate to reveal sensitive information at an open staff meeting, but key people may need to be taken into the professional circle of confidence.

The class tutor will already be fully appraised of the circumstances. Other staff who will teach the pupil, the special educational needs coordinator (SENCO) and senior managers should also be given a briefing. This should focus on issues raised at the induction meeting, on specific goals, on the pupil's additional needs and any domestic or personal circumstances which are relevant to understanding them, and should clearly explain any special arrangements or key strategies for managing the pupil.

Things to avoid

Perhaps the most serious mistake a school can inadvertently make is to protect the pupil from the consequences of their behaviour because they are 'different'. The objective should always be accountability with support. A pupil who is made accountable without being given support is being set up to fail. But it is collusive and usually self-defeating to give a pupil strong support without making them accountable for their behaviour.

Overcoming staff resistance

Members of staff may be resistant to the admission of children with problematic histories. The headteacher will need to:
* Make clear the school's responsibility to the community.
* Quash horror stories and exaggerated accounts of the pupil's past misdeeds.
* Hold talks with senior managers to work through their issues, and ensure they understand their responsibility to support agreed school policy on admissions and the importance to the community of this role.
* Make sure the school's policy on admissions, behaviour and pupil management recognises and reflects this essential community role. The policy should include clear guidance for staff on how incoming pupils should be managed.
* Make sure everyone understands that the pupil will be treated like any other and expected to keep the same standards of conduct in school.
* Do not live in denial. If some staff are hostile to the admission of a pupil, this should be dealt with at a special meeting involving those with concerns.

Some financial implications

Sources of funding for additional support vary widely in different localities. It could be a dowry payment from the excluding school to cover the remainder of that year's funding for the receiving school to use at its discretion or direct support through an intervention team (generally provided by psychological services or a mental health team), which would usually be accessed through the local authority. The school may be able to access additional money from government grants. Some local authorities help schools with additional funds for hard-to-place pupils.

The move could be part of an exchange arrangement where each school agrees to meet its own costs. Many schools have Behaviour Support Units or alternative on-site arrangements which are already funded directly or indirectly by government, and are able to meet the needs of the pupil without additional cash.

Case studies

Case study 1

Yassin, aged 14, was permanently excluded from an inner London school (something he admitted later he had provoked) and was enrolled at the local PRU which offered a specialist one- to two-term reintegration programme. Yassin was provided with six hours of one-to-one tuition and six hours of additional learning-related activities (with a support worker) per week, and regular sessions with a psychologist. Interventions included role play, speech therapy, specific accelerated learning targets, and home visits to help Mum learn to manage Yassin more effectively. Yassin often became anxious about his single mother and this explained his apparent school phobia.

After a number of sessions, Yassin realised he had to be a little less sensitive about what others might be thinking, and to avoid taking a confrontational stance toward teachers. He also had five months to mature, and to get very bored with the lack of friends and school life. His PRU programme was strictly one-to-one and did not involve dealing with groups and peer relationships. This approach reduces the need for staff to waste time managing group behaviours and increases the child's desire to return to school life.

When Yassin was reintegrated into a new mainstream school, his anxieties about his mother (who had critical health needs) were discussed at the induction meeting. It was agreed that Yassin could ask to go to the school office at any time and telephone his mother. He no longer had to feign tummy-aches or make trouble in order to get home and check on her well-being.

Yassin was too embarrassed to accept support in class even in his weak subjects, but did agree to meet with his support teacher after school several times a week.

Then unexpectedly, an attendance problem arose. Yassin's mother phoned the psychologist to say that he would not go to school again. A group of older boys, wearing hoodies, had followed him after school and he believed they were going to assault him. He could not identify them but 'One of them had a big knife in his pocket.' At this critical moment the bond of trust and mutual appreciation which had been developing between the mother and the psychologist was crucial. The psychologist was able to be honest about doubting the story – there were too many discrepancies – how did he know they were going to attack him, and had he actually seen the knife? She also carefully communicated that when children who were otherwise under the control of their parents did not attend school, it was nearly always because parents gave in to their entreaties when really they should have been firmer about setting boundaries. Yassin's mother put the phone down and went to talk to him. A few minutes later he came to the phone and said, 'I've decided, I am going back to school.'

That was it, there were no further problems and the support teacher was soon withdrawn.

Case study 2

David, 15, agreed to a managed move from his initial mainstream school to another. Although he started off well, old patterns of behaviour emerged. He had a reputation for angry outbursts in class which many teachers found intimidating and upsetting. He could also be argumentative, disruptive and confrontational. Staff were beginning to agitate for his removal from their school. In an effort to avoid this, the headteacher asked the psychologist who had facilitated the move to revisit the school and talk to all the teachers.

The psychologist met with each teacher in confidence. The agenda was two-fold: to help them understand David better, and to offer direct advice on effective strategies. The psychologist knew David's story well. Although he presented as a confident and powerful figure, there was another side to him. Underneath, David was unhappy, uncertain and insecure. He did not feel he belonged. One teacher described how she had lost her temper with him once and seen him '...deflate like a balloon. He looked pathetic and ashamed, and I felt guilty about reducing him to that state.'

The psychologist helped the teacher see that if she always recognised and talked to the real David within, rather than taking his obstreperous persona at face value, she would not lose her temper. She began to see that his behaviour was his own response to his feelings of insecurity and confusion, and that helping him to feel secure and wanted would pre-empt and resolve situations without the confrontations.

Hearing David's story made the teacher much more sympathetic to his hidden needs and changed the dynamics just enough to take the heat out of the situation. Fostering this combination of sympathy and attention to his real needs, rather than to his behaviour, was enough to achieve the headteacher's objectives. He found that, whilst David's behaviour didn't improve much in the short term, the teachers were more willing to work on their relationships with him and there were fewer complaints about him in the staff room.

Over time David started to feel he really did belong and that teachers seemed to like him. Gradually he found himself liking them in return, and because he was getting more help more quickly in class, the problems reduced.

Case study 3

Georgy, aged 13, had been taken in by a London school after being excluded. There was a lack of clarity and guidance from senior managers about his programme and the staff did not really want him in their classes (based on somewhat exaggerated and over-dramatised stories about him that the head-teacher did not quash). Minor transgressions of the rules were ignored, teachers tried to quarantine him rather than address his behaviour, which was naughty rather than dangerous. They turned a blind eye to so much that he came to feel that he could do what he wanted. As a result, his egotistical performances (designed mainly to impress his peers) became more flamboyant. Meanwhile, teachers began to dislike him and 'wish him elsewhere'.

But when another pupil told a teacher that Georgy had threatened her with a bottle the headteacher felt impelled to act. He called the parents in to a meeting which started badly and got worse. His mother was angry with the school because, as with previous meetings, the school was complaining to her but had not applied any sanctions on him. She made things worse by demanding to know if the school was going to permanently exclude him again. The headteacher answered 'Yes', seeming to act on impulse, and the mother stormed out of his office, searching for the teacher whom she thought had caused the problem. Ironically, another pupil kicked a teacher later that day, but the headteacher felt unable to permanently exclude two children on the same day, thus turning a blind eye to a physical assault on an adult. This story illustrates the need for scrupulous even-handedness and firm boundaries applied with consistency.

Case study 4

Yusuf became known as 'the invisible boy' to support workers. Yusuf was a 14-year-old Kurdish refugee who had a harrowing tale to tell about his long journey through Syria, Turkey and Germany to the UK. He laughingly described his art therapy sessions as follows: 'She didn't seem satisfied when I painted ordinary pictures, so I tried putting lots of red paint on and she liked that.' He had a reputation for threatening other children. His experiences had given him an outlook beyond his years. Nevertheless with support and therapy he was adjusting to life in the UK. Unfortunately, the headteacher and assistant headteacher at his school did not see eye-to-eye about integration, and the matter was never resolved between them. While the headteacher admitted the pupil, the assistant was determined to do nothing to support his induction. Yusuf was never added to the school database. He was expected to work in the library for many of his lessons and excluded from full participation. Any problems were dealt with summary rigidness.

Because Yusuf did not appear on the school roll, his support workers were unable to locate him when they came to the school and wasted most of their time trying to find someone who knew where he was. When the situation was relayed to the headteacher he passed the matter to his assistant who assiduously avoided dealing with it. At a meeting convened by the support team manager his position was immoveable – the placement 'was not working'.

Yusuf knew he was not wanted. The situation confirmed his worst views of his adoptive society. He voted with his feet by ensuring that his behaviour triggered further exclusion. The individualised programme which followed met his needs, but the education community had to bear the unnecessary cost of it.

3

FACILITATING MANAGED MOVES

Chapter 8

THE ROLE OF THE FACILITATOR

The facilitator's role is to understand the points of view of all parties involved in a situation which has led to a managed move. It is to bring them all together to negotiate a resolution which is satisfactory to everyone and which results in a suitable learning offer for the child whose needs cannot be met in their current school. This should be carried out with compassion and dispassion.

A good facilitator:
- Is everybody's friend. It is a position of minimal power and maximal influence.
- Works effectively within an emotionally charged environment to channel the emotion positively.
- Has good relational skills
- Understands the value of free reciprocal agreements.
- Never takes sides.
- Has good psychological and social awareness
- Has a unifying perspective

The success of a managed move largely depends on the nature of events, the location, and the cooperation of the participants. In particular, the therapeutic elements of the move require the pupil's cooperation. However, within these constraints the outcome rests on the facilitator's interpersonal skills and their ability to steer a process of change that carries people with it. A healthy sense of humour certainly helps.

What is on offer to the participants in a managed move is not 'the chance to meet someone else's needs', but 'the chance to meet my needs by cooperating with others to enable them to meet theirs.' In a successful managed move the pupil does not lose their sense of belonging to a caring community.

Everybody's friend
Friendship has human rather than professional connotations and the facilitator needs to express their humanity within professional boundaries. Facilitators who want to

form relationships with their clients quickly learn to put their own needs, as profes-sionals *and* as human beings, into the mixture. Doing so establishes an essential of restorative practice – commonality of interest.

Since reciprocity is a key lever in developing relationships of trust, it is important that feelings are expressed on both sides. Personal disclosures show children and parents in particular that the facilitator is on a level with them, not in an authority role. The concept of an internalised boundary is useful here. The facilitator knows which feelings and experiences are too sensitive to share with a client and which can be shared – for instance, every parent of teenage children has their angst story to tell.

Power and influence

The lack of power is no hindrance in a voluntary environment. More can be achieved through influence.

It is important to recognise antisocial and problematic behaviour as an indicator of unmet needs. Those who may have been wronged also have unmet needs for justice, reassurance, recompense, understanding, relief and closure. And there are the needs of the institution (expressed through the headteacher) for safety, security, good morale and ethos, and effective teaching.

The facilitator seeks to understand the underlying needs behind the positions people take up, and find ways to negotiate among the different groups so that every-one's needs are met to the greatest extent possible.

The facilitator needs to have skills and experience which range across psycho-logical, educational and welfare sectors. They are ideally placed to help different agen-cies involved in a managed move to communicate effectively. This inter-agency role is an active one, which involves the child and family in taking responsibility. We can think of it as 'bringing people closer to agencies that want to help, and agencies closer to the people they serve'.

The emotional environment

One very functional definition of emotions is 'internal experiences related to needs'. Good feelings follow when needs are met. Bad feelings develop when there are unmet needs.

Unfortunately, when people feel bad they do not generally ask themselves what need they have which is not being met. Instead the negative emotion is usually exter-nalised or projected. When a pupil's needs are not being met, the negative emotion expressed creates discord. It can also trigger a chain reaction of unmet needs in the teacher and other pupils.

Ultimately, this discord may also perform a useful function – breaking the rela-tionships holding that person in the group and releasing them to seek new groups where their needs *can* be met. A managed move can facilitate this process, or help the group find new ways to meet the needs of the marginalised person. Sometimes the pupil does not want a new opportunity in the same environment but in a new one. The problems may arise because the pupil is intuitively seeking a way out of a particular school situation. If the pupil can be helped to understand that they are creating a self-fulfilling prophecy, the situation can be reversed, with the school's support.

There are four ways that people externalise their feelings and they are all treated as a means of communication by facilitators:

- Verbal communication.
- Refractive response – so-called because the response is distorted from its origin.
- Non-verbal display of feelings in body language and behaviour.
- Non-verbal reaction – trying to make the other person feel what you are feeling.

Only the first method is generally effective. The others are likely to trigger defensive reactions.

For example, if a pupil feels angry with a teacher the best response is to say 'I feel angry' and explain why (verbal communication). A refractive response would be 'You are always picking on me.' Alternatively, the child might sit scowling with arms crossed (non-verbal display). Finally, the pupil might look for a way to make the teacher feel angry, using increasingly provocative tactics until the teacher shows they have got the message 'How do you like it when someone makes you angry?' (non-verbal reactive).

Relational skills can be used to translate these expressions of feeling from non-verbal to verbal form.

What are relational skills?

The term 'relational skills' means something more empathic and organic than 'inter-personal skills'. The purpose is to nurture positive relationships rather than to achieve aims.

Relational skills are primarily easy-to-learn language tools which enable people to create bonds of trust and cooperation quickly in the most difficult situations. They are a means of getting to the heart of the matter – the unmet needs and related feel-ings – and help facilitators balance the needs of professionals with those of young people, strengthening their own ability to hear others and respond effectively to hidden needs.

Relational skills also enable professionals to work effectively with angry or frus-trated children who are poor communicators, and to stimulate mutual respect. They enable the facilitator to handle awkward moments in the managed move conference and to diffuse tension before a crisis arises.

Relational skills work because they engage people on a fundamental level with two enduring human responses:

- 'We want to help.' Humans like to meet the needs of others. This is a product of social evolution. In effect, working together means meeting each other's needs.

- 'Your pain is our pain.' Humans do not like to see others in emotional distress. This is a function of 'we want to help'.

Free reciprocal agreements

People like to help each other within a reciprocal agreement: 'I will meet your needs if you meet my needs.' If we tell people what we need, and how our unmet need is making us feel, we create in them a powerful desire to help. When such agreements are freely given the relationship is balanced and mutually beneficial, allowing the development of positive regard and trust.

> Example:
> Jamie did not want to meet the psychologist making a home assessment. After 40 minutes he was still refusing to enter the room. Eventually he came in and sat down with his back to her and watched television, resolutely ignoring her. The psychologist said: 'When you sit with your back to me and ignore me, I feel anxious because I need to write a report that will help you. Will you turn round and talk to me?' Within five minutes the boy was chatting happily and showing her his pet gerbil. The psychologist was also happy that she could complete the assessment.

It sounds deceptively simple, and it works.

A good facilitator never takes sides

Being a facilitator is exciting and demanding. It is not easy to be with people in a supportive way and yet remain detached. It is all too easy to be swayed by one person's narrative, only to find the next participant's story sways sentiments the other way. It is better to have no sentiments at all. The facilitator's feelings about the historical facts are not relevant to the process. In this sense the facilitator should be invisible. Each participant is held in equal, unconditional, positive regard by the facilitator. The facilitator's own views and feelings about events should be discounted whilst in role. The facilitator's agenda is simply the narratives, needs, and feelings of the participants.

Psychological and social awareness

Facilitators try hard not to pathologise the situation. A functional approach is always best – what works, what doesn't work, and what learning needs are there? If mental health services have diagnosed a condition, syndrome or disorder, then this can assist in releasing extra funding or services, but will not help much in a managed move. So facilitators should not see themselves as meeting dysfunctional people; instead, they will meet 'human beings with some dysfunctional features'. A working knowledge of systemic family theory will help facilitators understand a family's boundaries, alliances and hierarchies and explore with them how things could be different.

Again, facilitators will meet children with features of autistic spectrum disorder, personality disorder, chronically poor social skills, mental health needs, and children who may be at-risk. It is essential to be familiar with the local child protection policy and not to be afraid to apply it if necessary.

It is useful to be aware of the ways in which people unconsciously project attitudes onto others and release pent-up feelings into unrelated situations. For instance, a headteacher may want to keep a pupil in school, but the pupil's teacher refuses to be reconciled with the child, not because of anything the child did (the explicit/ conscious reason) but because the teacher feels unsupported by the headteacher (implicit/ unconscious reason). The facilitator may be able to help the teacher to make this explicit – more support in class for the teacher could produce a change of heart.

A unifying perspective

A unifying perspective is very valuable. Some people find the following meditative exercise highly effective in centring their emotions, and in helping them hold multiple versions of the same events and respect the conflicting emotions of different parties. Contemplating these five truisms can help facilitators go into meetings, home visits and conferences in a receptive but neutral frame of mind. How it works is perhaps less important than the fact that it does.

The user focuses on a person or a group that they are about to meet and, if possible, each person is held in mind briefly. Then these five statements are repeated. Afterwards, a moment or two of quiet reflection will allow any intuitions arising from it to surface.

- Just like me, this person (or group) is seeking happiness in their lives.
- Just like me, this person (or group) is trying to avoid unhappiness in their lives.
- Just like me, this person (or group) has known sadness, loneliness and despair.
- Just like me, this person (or group) is seeking to meet their needs.
- Just like me, this person (or group) is learning about life.

Whether this or some alternative technique is used, a facilitator will work better if they develop the inner focus that enables them to intuit and connect with the needs and feelings of their clients.

Chapter 9

PROCESSES, DYNAMICS AND SCRIPTS

Facilitators should have a clear understanding of the difference between a process and a structure. A process is a series of procedural steps driven by dynamics. A structure is something that is fixed – for instance, the mandatory elements of the education system. Processes can lead to real change. To achieve this, the managed move process must involve choice, and engender a sense of participation.

Dynamics are created when a person anticipates that they will experience positive feelings by achieving an attainable goal. A thirsty person, on seeing a glass of water, is driven towards it, anticipating the cool liquid in their throat. The facilitator creates dynamics in the participants involved in a managed move by helping them identify their needs and by showing them how to attain them.

The participants in a managed move have complex and volatile needs. The facilitator has to balance these, always mindful of the four values: respect for equal opportunities, attention to the needs of others, promotion of voluntariness and choice, and appreciative and accepting enquiry. To do so, scripts have been developed which the facilitator uses as signposts and safe havens throughout the process.

Unlike a stage script, managed move scripts only specify the words used by the facilitator. Using a predetermined script will not inhibit the process. When emotions arise at a managed move meeting, whether it is anger or tearfulness, it is surprising how effective using a script can be in moving things forward in the right direction.

The process of a managed move entails both group and individual work. The group work, which involves bringing together diverse people who may have strong feelings about a recent event, is a bit like organising a party, with the facilitator acting as host and making sure every guest is happy. The facilitator also works one-to-one with the narratives of each person.

Working with narratives

The narrative thread is the story each person chooses to tell about the situation leading up to the managed move conference. By connecting with the underlying needs and feelings expressed in the narrative, the facilitator is able to modify it. As this process takes place with each participant, the narrative threads begin to connect. At the conference, as each person's narrative is heard, and if the facilitator has been able to bring the threads nearly into alignment, the sense of mutual understanding acts like a magnet to bring people into consensus.

From the Maori culture in New Zealand, from which restorative justice sprang, comes a saying which sums this up perfectly: 'There is but one eye of the needle through which passes the black thread, the white thread and the red thread.' The process of restorative justice has the effect of enabling people to come, like the black, red and white threads, to the eye of the needle and to pass through in union.

How the narrative is reshaped

A facilitator will create a map of narratives, needs and feelings. This map is a dynamic one in that it changes. The changes are driven by new realisations and new information channelled into the process by the facilitator.

The facilitator simply asks the participants about their feelings, needs and requests, using the scripts provided, and explores their responses. When reviewing and summarising the situation the facilitator makes these the key points and rearranges other elements of the story around them.

When politicians in Northern Ireland finally sat down together it was because they had reached agreement about one thing – both sides shared a common vision of peace with justice. When two parties start moving towards a common goal together, it is hardly surprising if they arrive together too.

However small the area of overlapping need, and hence agreement, it is the 'safe haven' from which all progress will flow, as people start to focus on their common hopes and visions.

The process of remapping, or reshaping, the narrative takes place with each participant. If a participant's narrative were to be written down in graphic form, it would usually start off looking like a particularly mad brainstorm. The narrator's perspective on events needs to be respected but not sanctified. The facilitator wants to hear another version which has three elements: feelings, needs and requests.

At first the narrative is full of clutter, such as moral judgements and feelings projected onto others. Other participants can become objectified, classified and

derided. There may be true but unhelpful comparisons and a general insensitivity to the feelings and needs of wrong-doers. The problem with narratives in their raw form is that other parties will feel attacked by them, and react defensively. Feelings and needs are obscured, and may not be mentioned at all.

The facilitator unravels this conglomeration to make the feelings, needs and requests of each participant explicit and to locate all the other material in this context. Without losing any of the concerns expressed by the narrator the facilitator is now able to help them reframe their position. How much they are willing to change is up to them. It may take time for them to think things through; they may even need a second meeting.

Requests are demands expressed in cooperative language. For instance, 'He can't come back to this school' becomes 'We think another school will meet his needs better and we would like you to consider a managed move.' 'I hate the teacher and behave badly because he picks on me' becomes 'I get very frustrated because I need more help with this subject and would like to be moved to another group where I can get the help I need.' The changes may sound prosaic or cosmetic, but in the context of a conference such requests are more likely to produce positive reactions.

Bringing the narratives together

Now that the narratives are defined by the feelings, needs and requests of each partici-pant they fit together more easily. Since participants can rightly own them, they are less judgemental and condemning and so less contentious. Contrast 'You are a disrup-tive influence and I want you out' with 'When you walk around and talk to others in the class I feel frustrated and annoyed because I cannot teach, and I would like you to move to a place which suits your learning needs better.'

The term 'requests' includes hopes, aspirations, expectations and wishes. It is surprising how much agreement is easily found in the requests of participants. The headteacher may want to see the back of a pupil, but they also want to see the pupil go to a place where their learning needs can be met. The parents and child want the same. Everyone wants the child to be happy and to learn.

If the issues can be shared in a non-blaming atmosphere then there is every reason for agreement. Because the school does not need to make a case against the child, there is reduced emphasis on wrong-doing and punishment and greater emphasis on what the child (and the community) needs.

The objective is to meet everybody's requests in one way or another, with a degree of compromise, and in doing so to form the content of the agreement.

Key points to remember about the process
- It gives the aggrieved a chance to say what they want or need.
- Wherever possible, everyone who has been affected should be heard.
- The emphasis is on restoration rather than punishment.
- Retributive dynamics should be reframed as requests for reparation.

- The wrong-doer is made fully accountable for their actions, whilst being fully supported by professionals and family.
- Children should be given the opportunity to make up for what has happened.
- Reparation needs to be real.
- Adults including professionals should acknowledge it if they have contributed to the problems in any way.

Creating the right dynamics

Motivation is goal-directed, and goals are visionary – they exist in the future and are as yet unrealised. The facilitator, in the simplest possible way, enables participants to look at the situation differently, by proposing new goals and reminding participants of goals they may have forgotten.

When the predominant dynamic in a managed move situation is 'move the child away' then results may be mixed. When the dynamic is 'find a place for the child where their needs *are* met' the results are likely to be much better.

The participants' visions are, initially, likely to be problem-focused and not solution-focused. A good facilitator assertively changes dynamics that can be changed, calmly accepts those which cannot, and wisely knows which is which.

If we want people to change, the internal motives of the participants are all-important. The facilitator helps the participants change their narratives and this changes the dynamics.

For instance, when someone does something wrong they know it. When they are punished they feel they have paid the price. Therefore, 'Those who do the crime must do the time' is not very constructive. Better to say: 'Those who do social harm should be expected to repair the harm done.'

This is restorative justice. It is achieved by inviting participants to review their primary goals. This means replacing problem-focused goals with solution-focused ones.

Problem-focused goal	Solution-focused goal
School	*School*
Getting the pupil out	Moving the pupil on
Finding out what is 'wrong' with the pupil	Finding out what the pupil's 'whole learning' needs are
Explaining what the pupil has done wrong	Requiring an explanation from the pupil for their behaviour
Getting the pupil to admit they were wrong	Helping the pupil understand cause and effect in their lives
Deciding the appropriate punishment	Requiring appropriate reparation

Parents	*Parents*
Stopping the headteacher from excluding their child	Ensuring the child has the right learning opportunity
Blaming the school	Asking the school to understand their point of view

Pupil	*Pupil*
Regretting what has been lost	Seeking the best possible outcome
Denying or defending behaviour	Explaining and taking responsibility for their actions
Blaming the school	Being grown-up and acknowledging the harm done
Feeling sorry for themselves	Offering reparation
Avoiding painful issues	Clearing the air
Trying to hide their perceived failings	Recognising and asking for what they need

How to use scripts

If only three words were available to the facilitator, they would be **'Who needs what?'** This is the solution-focused question which replaces 'What is wrong?'

The word 'script' has dramatic connotations, as in a play. Indeed, getting involved in the real-life drama of the child is a challenge every facilitator must face. This applies to all participants, but adults usually have a better grasp of reality than children and are less likely to hold incoherent or fantastic views. Children sometimes find it more difficult to distinguish between their inner and outer worlds and when they are in trouble they often project their problems onto other people, blaming others and feeling helpless.

There are at least five good reasons for using scripts:

1   They cover all aspects of the process comprehensively in a minimum of words.
2   They provide a safety net if and when emotions make the atmosphere at the managed move conference sensitive or volatile.
3   Their use makes participants feel secure.
4   They make the facilitator feel secure.
5   There are plenty of opportunities for the unexpected to occur. The script acts as a continuous point of reference to bring participants back to the process.

Even experienced facilitators need to take a summary of the script to the conference and refer to it. This removes an unnecessary additional stressor – remembering what comes next.

There is one main script, the conference script, from which fragments are taken for use in meetings and home visits. This script has a few key variants. You can modify the script once you get used to it.

Facilitators use the same script with everybody, and this has a unifying effect. Each participant is also asked a number of key questions which are applicable only to them. In effect, the facilitator uses the scripts to:

- Hear the narrative of each participant.
- Work this material into a map of feelings, needs and requests.
- Rehearse what each participant is likely to say at the managed move conference.

This is achieved by asking the participants the same questions they will be asked at the conference.

The scripts for acute and chronic situations are nearly the same. The questions cover:

- What happened?
- How are things now?
- What are your hopes for the future?

The core script[30]

The core of the script provides a framework for the various meetings and for the conference itself.

What happened?

What thoughts did you have at the time?

How did you feel about the incident then?

What effect has the situation had on you?

Who else has been affected by the situation?

How were they affected?

What has happened since the situation occurred?

How do you feel about the situation now?

How are things now?

What do you think should happen now?

How can the harm done be repaired?

How can we work to prevent the situation arising again?

What other needs remain to be met?

Are you willing to come to a conference and share what you have been saying with (list expected participants)?

What do you hope to see come out of this conference?

30 Adapted with thanks from the model conference script used by Minnesota Department of Corrections, St Paul, Minnesota, USA 55108–5219, with technical assistance from the National Institute of Corrections.

This script fragment is carefully worded so that it is applicable to all participants, although of course the tone changes depending on their status.

Whether a conference results in a managed move or not:

- Everyone moves on afterwards.
- Changes are made on all sides.
- Adults and professionals find ways to bring about change for the aggrieved and the wrong-doer.

Chapter 10

RELATIONAL SKILLS

'It's not squash, it's tennis!'

Relational skills quickly build a relationship of trust and mutual confidence with common goals. Sometimes professionals act like the walls of a squash court: if the child hits a high one it goes out. Contrast this with the way a good tennis coach works with a young player. The child hits the ball all over the place and the coach returns it each time to exactly the right place, so that the child finds it easier to practice the correct stroke.

Relational skills enable facilitators to act in a similar way, bringing hidden needs to the surface, enabling children to voice their real wishes and concerns, and reframing things in a more positive way. The four main skills are:
- Active listening.
- Asking open-ended questions.
- Cognitive interview techniques.
- Non-violent communication.

It is useful to remember that the facilitator is never in the role of adjudicator. Meetings are a friendly dialogue not a psychological assessment or intervention.

The application of these skills is most effective when the user has an understanding of people, a sense of humility, a good grasp of the values and principles supporting their work, a strong sense of empathy, powerful intuition, a smooth tongue, and a spirited love of enquiry.

However, the techniques can be applied by anyone. So much can be learned by practice, simply by following the recommended syntax, sticking to the preferred vocabulary, and doing things in the right order. All the virtues listed above will be learned through experience, and the only one needed from the start is humility – so that one can learn from mistakes!

Active listening[31]

Active listening has four components:

* Actively listening and reflecting back the last statement of the participant.
* Actively listening and asking the participant for clarification of a statement.
* Summarising a longer passage of conversation.
* Reviewing and rephrasing a whole conversation and asking the participant if they agree with the review.

Active listening skills are fundamental. They require us to respect the individual and their right to self-determination. They make people feel they have really been listened to and help the speaker order their thoughts and be clear about what they feel and what they need.

When we try to persuade someone to change their views it is often perceived as an attack on their self-image, and produces defensive responses which become points of disagreement. In doing so we are responding to our own needs or the needs of other participants.

Active listening means hearing and responding to the free expressions of others, without articulating negative or positive opinions. It is an enquiry after their truth. In so enquiring, we may help the speaker notice inconsistencies of logic and unhelpful attitudes in their story which they may choose to reframe. By listening and responding with full attention to the words and feelings expressed, and sensing what lies behind them, the facilitator conveys their unconditional positive regard for the speaker, or empathy.

Active listening carries a degree of personal risk. If we sense deeply the feelings of another person and understand the meaning their experiences have for them, we risk being changed ourselves. As the American psychologist Carl Rogers said: 'It is threatening to give up, even momentarily, what we believe and start thinking in someone else's terms. It takes a great deal of inner security and courage to be able to risk one's self in understanding another.'[32]

The facilitator needs to maintain a healthy internalised boundary between their professional role, *with all its human connotations*, and their own personal and private humanity. In short, on one side of the boundary is the person in the role of facilitator, engaging on a human level but in a professional capacity, while on the other side there is calm and detachment.

There is a fine line between these positions. Facilitators usually have regular supervision and this is an opportunity to explore this aspect of their work. Facilitators need to protect their sense of humour, try not to let things get out of proportion and shouldn't take their work home.

---

31 O. Egan, *The Skilled Helper: A problem-management approach to helping*, 6th edn (Pacific Grove, California, Brooks/Cole Publishing, 1998).

32 C. Rogers and R.E. Farson, 'Active Listening' (1957), in *Communicating in Business Today*, ed. R.G. Newman, M.A. Danziger and M. Cohen (Lexington, Mass., D.C. Heath and Co., 1987).

Asking open-ended questions

A question is open-ended if it draws out the participant and is hard to answer with a yes or a no. Questions that start with How, Why, What, Which and Who are usually open-ended.

It is a good idea to ask politely, and not interrogatively, and to invite the participant to 'tell', 'explain', 'help me understand', 'give me the lowdown on', 'shed some light'. Facilitators might ask:

- 'Would you tell me about ...?'
- 'Please explain that bit about ...'
- 'What about the ... , can you shed some light on that for me, please?'

These phrases can be quite long, and convey a great deal of warmth and respect, and still be no more than actively listening and reflecting back or asking for clarification of a single statement. Making the phrases long gives the participant time to relax and absorb the fuller meaning, to clarify their responses, and to feel really listened to. This is a powerful dynamic for change.

- 'I find it hard to understand that. It worries me a bit because I know you want to sort out this situation, and I do too, but it just struck me as odd. Would you please explain what you meant when you said ...?'

Cognitive interview techniques[33]

Cognitive interview techniques are widely used by police interviewers to generate additional evidence, primarily with witnesses.

These techniques are designed to help the interviewee immerse themselves in their memory and recover forgotten elements of their narrative.

- The interviewer helps the interviewee enter a calm and internally focused state and remember all the details of an event, whether or not they seem relevant.
- Events are reviewed as an uninterrupted narrative from as near the 'beginning of the event' as the participant chooses up to the present time.
- The interviewer now reviews the whole narrative starting from the present and working backwards, building up the most complete picture possible at each point in time and linking the pictures across the time line.
- The interviewer makes a point of closing the interview and making sure the participant does not have any unresolved feelings about what can be a vivid and realistic internal journey through memory.

This approach can help a respondent get in touch with the feelings and thoughts which preceded a crisis. It is effective because memory works by association. For example, asking a student about the details of break-time football may remind them

---

33 R.P. Fisher and R.E. Geiselman, *Memory-enhancing Techniques for Investigative Interviewing: The cognitive interview* (Illinois, Thomas Springfield, 1992).

that they were feeling annoyed with another student at the start of a lesson, and help explain the problems which arose later.

Non-violent communications[34]

- Other people do not 'make' us feel things.
- When other people trigger negative feelings, we can usually find out which of our unmet needs the feelings relate to.
- It is safe to be honest about this when asking people to change.

Marshall Rosenberg, founder and director of educational services at the Center for Nonviolent Communication in America, describes an open expression of feeling and need as 'giraffe language' (gentle with big ears) in contrast to 'jackal-speak'. His language formula enables people to say difficult things in a way that can be heard and to invite changes of behaviour or a different response to questions.

A non-violent communication (NVC) statement contains:

Observations
State the observations without judgement, evaluation or comment: 'The head-teacher tells me you caused problems in class' becomes 'The headteacher says that on three occasions you walked out of the classroom without permission.'

Feelings
State the negative feelings this engendered, whether in the teacher, the head-teacher or yourself.

Needs
Explain the unmet needs the feelings represent – in terms of the harm done by the events, or your own need for understanding.

Requests
Make a request for something specific which will meet the unmet need you have – which could simply be for more information expressed as specifically as possible.

This core NVC technique has its own mnemonic: 'NVC works oftener' – that's OFNR. Take a moment to test your spontaneous reaction to the following three remarks, and compare how you would feel if they were said to you:

'You never listen!!'

'You are not listening!'

'When you turn round in your seat I worry that you are not listening.'

Once you have understood basic NVC skills you can start translating other people's 'jackal-speak' into 'giraffe language' and so work out their needs and requests:

'When you said "this conference is rubbish" were you feeling anxious that the conference would not listen to your side of the story?'

---

34 With thanks to Marshall Rosenberg. M.B. Rosenberg, *Nonviolent Communication: A language of life* (California, Puddle Dancer Press, 2004 [www.cnvc.org]).

Chapter 11

SETTING UP A MANAGED MOVE CONFERENCE

Check-list

Preliminary stage:

- Take referral from the school's headteacher or deputy, and concerned teachers.
- Begin to draw up a guest list for the managed move conference with contact details and any comments or notes and keep this up to date.
- Meet with and thoroughly prepare each of the primary participants – aggrieved and wrong-doer (usually home visits).
- Confirm their voluntary agreement to meet with all those concerned and discuss how, realistically, to repair the harm done and what should happen in the future.
- If the aggrieved has actual (quantifiable) losses, ask them to list these and discuss possible forms of reparation. As regards non-quantifiable harm, ask them what might satisfy their need for a just outcome.
- Make sure the primary participants are sufficiently supported.
- Consider involving those affected by the situation (classmates, family, co-workers, police officers, neighbours), contacting them by phone or in person. If you decide they should be invited make sure they understand it is voluntary.
- Consider involving professionals who have an interest in the outcome of the conference or who are involved in the comprehensive assessment (see pages 53–4), especially the headteacher of the 'receiving' school, college or Pupil Referral Unit (PRU), social workers, local authority representation, probation officer, police officers and Youth Offending Team – contacting them by phone or in person. If you decide they should be invited make sure they understand it is voluntary. Don't overload the conference with adults.

- Consider inviting only the key people – small conferences can work well too. However, it is usually considered best to invite 'everyone involved'.
- Send an invitation letter, with date, time, venue and your mobile phone number, *and obtain confirmation*. A neutral venue, such as a community centre, library or meeting room is normally used. Send guests a map or 'how to get there' information, if necessary.

Before the conference:
- Consider whether everyone attending has sufficient information and has agreed to any changes to the plan or guest list.
- Review the attitudes, feelings and personalities each individual may bring to the conference.
- Consider strategies to pre-empt problems.
- Check all arrangements for hosting – location, chairs, refreshments, travel arrangements for guests (organise transport if necessary), access, child-care issues. If a board or flipchart is necessary to record key points and agreements, check its availability. Get tissues for those who may become emotional.
- Review any special needs or cultural concerns of the participants.
- Some participants may require a reassuring telephone call on the day.
- Think through the likely progress of the conference and the need for any special introductions, rules or other concerns.
- Consider the seating plan – you may have a sense of who will be angry or distracting or feel isolated and who will be supportive.
- Think about the order in which you will invite people to introduce themselves – in some cultures this is important.
- Consider opening statements carefully. Preferably while resting quietly without distractions, compassionately consider the needs of each participant.

The referral

Gather the name and contact details of the referrer (i.e. the headteacher), any other professionals involved, and the name and contact details of pupil and family, pupil's age and school year. Ask to see any key documents if these are not offered (although this is not a paper-driven exercise).

Agree with the headteacher how the family will be contacted – usually the school asks the parents to meet with the facilitator via the exclusion or managed moves letter (see pages 46–51), and gives the facilitator the contact details to follow up.

Use the core script to explore the situation, and clarify the real needs and expectations of the headteacher. Additionally, always ask:
- 'Under what circumstances would a return to school become possible for this pupil?'

Another good question is:
- 'If I could guarantee the problems will not recur, would you consider a return to school?'

If the answer is yes, discuss how this might be achieved.

If it is no, the family will need to understand that their choices are reduced to agreeing a managed move or dealing with the consequences of a permanent exclusion and possible appeal. Although this might not sound much of a choice, it does provide an opportunity to negotiate the terms of the move and for the pupil to resolve outstanding business and move on positively.

In initiating the managed move process, the headteacher may have:
- Decided to make up their mind at the conference whether to ask for a managed move.
- Decided to ask for a managed move but is not sure whether to permanently exclude if the parents do not agree to a move.
- Made up their mind that if the parents do not agree to a move they will permanently exclude.
- Already permanently excluded the pupil, or be about to do so.

In a critical situation, the headteacher's hand may be forced. In a chronic situation, there is often more room for manoeuvre.

Always ask:
- 'What are the good things about this pupil?'
- 'What does he or she do well?'
- 'What are their strengths?'
- 'Who likes them and why?'

It is important to draw in these positive affirmations, which the pupil can aspire to build on. 'Catch them being good' is a cliché – but a useful one.

The unresolved feelings of staff and other pupils may impede a successful return to school. If possible, it is best to include someone in the conference to represent the views of the staff, and/or of the pupils, to allow their feelings to be addressed.

The home visit

In an acute situation there is nearly always at least one aggrieved person, usually a pupil or teacher. Occasionally the offence is against the community as a whole (graffiti for instance), in which case the headteacher or their delegate represents the community. Managed moves are often triggered by a series of less serious critical incidents and it is useful to involve the aggrieved from the most recent one.

So there is always one home visit to the wrong-doer, and usually but not always one to the aggrieved. Parents can be given the managed move information sheet (pages 37–8) before or during the visit.

The home visit should help the family begin to move on. An hour spent with them in the home can achieve more than months of simmering watchfulness and professional concern. Empathise, explore strengths and weaknesses, offer expert opinion and support. Voice your concerns clearly using non-violent language. Set clear parameters for the family's expectations.

The home visit can dramatically change the picture. The school report may describe abusive language, hitting people, and shouting at the teacher. But the pupil describes himself as a shy boy who finds it hard to get to sleep, gets upset at home and wants to change. The visit reveals that he sleeps in the front room, has trouble understanding instructions, frequently gets confused and has an abusive father.

Facilitators should use the core script as the basic interview framework for the meeting. The facilitator will have already learned the headteacher's position. However, it is always possible that the headteacher may change their mind and consider some alternative to a managed move. In advising parents of the position, the facilitator must judge how to balance hope and realism.

A child or parent may want to nominate a supporter – a friend to accompany them at the managed move conference. If so, any transport or care conflicts will need to be addressed. Be inclusive, be realistic, if necessary make the ground rules for the meeting very clear, and ask possible participants to confirm their agreement at the home visit.

The family may be facing other difficulties, such as bereavement or family breakdown. Parents may have unresolved feelings about their own schooling. There may be confusion about the parents' rights. The facilitator must make sure the options are fully explained.

Seeing the child alone

The facilitator needs a chance to talk to the child on his or her own. It is better not to see them at school before the home visit so that they don't associate the facilitator with the authority of the school. Once a relationship has been initiated this will be less of a problem.

The home visit can provide an opportunity for a one-to-one chat. If appropriate, ask the parents to absent themselves for a period at the beginning of the meeting, especially if the child is older. Facilitators can also talk with the child later in the visit or afterwards by meeting them at school or after school at a café or other public venue where it is possible to talk in private.

For a team-based facilitator, there are advantages in working with a colleague. However, this is no reason to avoid working alone, including doing home visits and meeting with older children outside of school and home. If circumstances dictate that the facilitator is, for instance, alone in a car with a young person, it is important scrupulously to maintain physical distance and not to say or do anything that might be misinterpreted. If an appropriate friendship has been formed with the pupil, the likelihood of a problem is minimal, since they will know the facilitator is trying to help.

Children in trouble may have some combination of learning deficits, unhelpful attitudes and beliefs, peer-group problems, poor social and relational skills, uncertainty about identity, low self-esteem, power and control conflicts, or confusion over sexuality. The facilitator uses relational skills to explore these difficulties, and develops a list of functional needs (such as language skills development, or anger management training) which should be addressed in the agreement made at the conference.

Children at risk of school failure persistently use social strategies which are naive, ineffective and offensive. As a result they may find themselves rejected by others, subject to sanctions, and unable to achieve goals. Facing a managed move sometimes helps them to look at their behaviour in a new light.

A facilitator might ask the child 'Can you think of any other way you might have dealt with the situation?' and 'What might have happened if you had done this or that?' Children often respond better to such questions in an informal one-to-one setting.

Hidden needs

Children have a strong sense of justice. If they believe they have been treated unjustly or unequally, it can be a major sticking point. But the conference will give them a chance to explain their feelings, and this can build a bridge to a successful resolution.

A pupil who feels they have been unfairly or harshly treated by a member of staff will feel resentful. If their resentment is expressed refractively or non-verbally (see page 72), it causes more friction, and turns the aggrieved child into a wrong-doer. The child then feels the injustice all the more, caught in a vicious circle which began when their original claims of unfair treatment went unheeded by the community.

In one London comprehensive, the headteacher kept a red book outside his office door and any pupil with a complaint against staff could write this in it. Every complaint was followed up and the vast majority provided object lessons in social skills and awareness for the pupil. Just occasionally, the headteacher found an adult could have dealt with things better, and in a quiet meeting with pupil and staff member the issue was explored in a non-blaming way, lessons learned on all sides and the matter closed.

Some needs are hidden only because the relevant information had never been collected.

Example:
A primary pupil who was not able to stay on task, hid under tables, and sometimes ran out of school and went home was causing the school great concern. After patient outreach work, the facilitator discovered a history of family bereavement. The boy believed his mother had the same illness that had caused his aunt's sudden death. His father had been imprisoned twice and the boy knew he might disappear again. It was not surprising that he was too anxious to be in school. Once this hidden need was exposed, services rallied round to support the whole family.

Other needs are hidden because they are embarrassing. For instance, one mother had trouble admitting she had not attended meetings because they took place the day before her girocheque arrived and she did not have the bus fare. Some professionals viewed her as 'a poor attender'. Once she could open up to the facilitator, shared understanding altered the perspective of all those concerned.

Sometimes needs are hidden because they relate to dark secrets, such as child abuse, that the facilitator will have to take responsibility for sharing more widely. Child protection guidelines are very clear about this and facilitators should know their own agency's policy and practice.[35] The safety of children takes precedence over any ethical concerns about confidentiality.

There are two fundamental rules: don't try to investigate allegations yourself (listen to any narrative but don't ask probing questions) and you must inform the nearest Social Services or police child protection team if you have concerns about the safety of a child or vulnerable adult. If your organisation has a designated key person whose job this is, you can inform them instead. (Make a record of how you did this.)

The following confidentiality statement reassures the client that they will have a say in any disclosures whilst protecting their reasonable right to privacy. Use it at the start of your engagement with children or parents:

'Everything you say to me is said "in confidence". That means I will not tell anybody things you ask me to keep private. And if you tell me anything which makes me worry that a child[36] may be at risk of being harmed, I will tell you about my worries and we can decide together who else needs to know.'

Other agencies

A number of agencies might be involved in a managed move conference, and their narratives will also be collected. It can be a good idea to meet them in an informal setting, but usually time constraints restrict this to a telephone conversation.

If you have carried out a comprehensive assessment (see pages 53–4) as well as preparing for the conference, you will need to discuss the issues arising from this with the relevant agencies and establish how the additional needs identified will be met.

There is one agency which must be involved in the managed move conference – the receiving agency, whether this is a school, a PRU, a short-term intervention programme, or an individualised home and community programme.

---

35 *What to do if you're worried a child is being abused* (London, HMSO, 2006),
   http://publications.teachernet.gov.uk/eOrderingDownload/6840-DfES-IFChildAbuse.pdf, and *Working Together to Safeguard Children* (London, DfES, 2006), http://www.everychildmatters.gov.uk/workingtogether/
36 Add 'or vulnerable person' if any of the families involved may include such persons.

Chapter 12

FACILITATING THE CONFERENCE

Overview of the conference running order
    Introductions
    Hearing the narratives
    Making the agreement
        What reparation is needed?
        Is a managed move needed?
        What is the alternative learning offer?
        Will the parents agree to a managed move?
    Closing the conference

The script for a managed move conference which has a justice theme (usually when a critical event has occurred) is slightly different from that of a family theme (usually when there is a chronic situation).

The main difference between the two types of conference is that a justice theme focuses on reparation, reconciliation and commitment by a wrong-doer not to repeat the same behaviour. If the conference involves two people who are *both* wrong-doers and aggrieved, the harm done tends to be cancelled out. A family theme needs to focus more on support and intervention. Since there is often a dual theme, the two versions may have to be blended. Remember that changes in opportunity (from the community) and changes in outlook (from the child and family) go together, and should be balanced.

The wrong-doer is always a pupil, but the aggrieved may be a pupil or pupils, parents, teachers or other professionals. The wrong-doing might have been directed at the school, making it the aggrieved party. In this case, the headteacher represents the school community.

Treat each aggrieved party in the same way, making age- and status-appropriate adjustments as required. Professionals are considered as supporters of both the wrong-doer and the aggrieved.

If the child or parent has chosen to invite a friend to the meeting to support them they can still contribute even if they were not involved in the matters under discussion. Their views are often pivotal.

Introductions

Welcome the participants to the building and offer refreshments.

Seat the different parties separately (if this seems a good idea) before inviting them into the conference room and then seating them according to your seating plan.

If the seats are carefully placed in an exact circle it creates a powerful sense of equal status and equal inclusion. It is also interesting to see when someone moves their chair slightly out of the circle.

Open the conference:

* *Thank you for coming to this meeting. My name is _____ , and I will be facilitating this conference. Before beginning I would like each person to introduce themselves and to say how they would like to be addressed.*

You need to remember each person's choice. Invite professionals to use their given name, if possible.

(Justice theme)

* *Something happened that made a lot of people hurt and angry.*
* *(Name) has admitted their part in the events.*
* *The meeting will focus on what they did (have been doing) and how their behaviour has affected others.*

OR

(Family theme)

* *There have been a number of problems in school which are causing concern.*
* *(Name) has agreed their part in these problems.*
* *The meeting will focus on what has happened (has been happening) and how their behaviour has affected others.*

Describe the situation in less than 50 words.

* *We are not here to decide whether they are good or bad people.*
* *This is an opportunity to repair any harm that has been done and work to prevent this happening again.*
* *We will also see what else is needed to support the young people involved.*
* *Everyone will have their say without interruption and have other people listen to them with respect.*
* *After everyone has had their say I will make sure that you have a chance to ask*

questions or respond to what others have said.
- *We hope to end the conference by reaching agreement about what should be done to repair the harm done and prevent it happening again.*
- *We want an agreement that will bring positive outcomes for all, and enable us to decide on the next steps.*
- *Each of us will be expected to keep the terms of the agreement.*
- *My role is to facilitate this meeting and keep this a safe place for all of you to express yourselves.*
- *I would like to remind everyone that they may choose to end their participation at any time – this is a voluntary meeting.*
- *Does that seem fair to everyone? Have I said clearly why we are here?*

Check with each person, usually by eye contact.

The narratives

Now the participants give their narratives in response to the relevant core script questions which you may have rehearsed with them.

Even if you have not met the supporters before, still go through the questions in the core script with them.

Usual order of participants:
- Wrong-doer.
- Aggrieved (the headteacher goes last on behalf of the school).
- Supporters of the aggrieved.
- Supporters of the wrong-doer.
- Professionals.

Ask each in turn:
- *What happened /How did you hear about what happened/What sorts of problem have there been?*
- *What thoughts did you have at the time?*
- *How did you feel about the situation (problems) then?*
- *What effect has the situation had on you?*
- *Who else has been affected by the situation?*
- *How were they affected?*
- *What has happened since the situation (problems) occurred?*
- *How do you feel about the situation (problems) now?*
- *What do you think should happen now?*
- *What do you want to see come out of this conference?*

Supporters and professionals may be asked only questions they can relevantly answer. Questions about feelings are almost always relevant.

Address the following questions to the relevant pupil(s):

(Justice theme)
- *You have just listened to everybody and heard how they have been affected by what you did (what has happened) and the harm that has been caused. Is there anything you wish to say?*
- *Do you see that the choices you made and what you have done have caused harm?*
- *At the start you said you thought (name) had been affected. Can you add to those who have been affected by your actions?*
- *Is there anything you would like to say to anyone at this point?*

OR

(Family theme)
- *You have just listened to everybody and heard how they have been affected or harmed by the things that have happened. Is there anything you wish to say?*
- *Do you see that the choices you made helped to cause this?*
- *At the start you said you thought (name) had been affected. Can you add to those who have been affected by your actions?*
- *Is there anything you would like to say to anyone at this point?*

Wait quietly to allow the pupil(s) time to make apologies, express remorse or contrition, or explain themselves further.

(Only if appropriate)
Address the following question to the aggrieved:
- *You have heard what (name) has to say. Is there anything you would like to say in return?*
- *Would you like to shake hands with (name)?*

If the answer is yes, check with the wrong-doer for assent, and then facilitate this. Alternatively, the conference may flow better if there is an opportunity for apologies during the next section.

Making the agreement
What reparation and support are needed?
This part of the conference will be more open-ended. In particular make sure that all parties have a chance to be conciliatory. Apologies and handshakes are the norm but are not usually sufficient on their own to achieve this. Reparation should be as concrete as possible.

Consider the support needs of any aggrieved parties as well as the support needs of the wrong-doer. The alternative learning offer, which will be drawn up into an individual education plan (IEP), should include the wrong-doer's support package.

Compensation may be offered, in kind or cash. Community service in school or other positive social contributions may be carried out. The wrong-doer may offer to speak to peers or make a public apology, and if they are peer-leaders (this is not unusual) they can offer to ensure the safety and security of aggrieved parties in and around the school. Symbolic acts of reparation should be seen by the aggrieved as significant.

Ask each person:

- *It is important we now consider what needs to happen to repair the harm done as much as possible. What do you think is the right and fair thing to do to repair the harm?*
- *What else do we need to do to support the pupil(s) involved today? (Repeat if necessary to gather more ideas.)*

As before, begin with the wrong-doer, followed by the aggrieved. It is then usual to go to the supporters of the aggrieved and the supporters of the wrong-doer. Where one of the aggrieved parties is a teacher or other professional, it is probably best to hear them after any family members. The headteacher of the school (or their delegate) goes last, since their view about the managed move is paramount.

Is a managed move needed?

- *I come now to you (name of headteacher). You have heard everything that has happened here. What reparation do you think is appropriate and what else do you think needs to be done?*

A support and intervention package will be needed whether or not there will be a managed move.

What is the alternative learning offer?

- *(Name of representative of alternative learning setting), what can you offer (name of pupil) and (name of parent(s)) as an alternative learning offer?*

Once the alternative learning offer has been described, a discussion may ensue. The facilitator should ensure that all the pupil's learning needs have been addressed. The offer may be extended and some parts may be provisional. These will also be added to the agreement, creating an obligation in good faith to fulfil them.

If the headteacher has decided the pupil can return to school with more support and an intervention package, close the conference. Otherwise continue.

Will the parents agree to a managed move?

The facilitator summarises the proposed action plan and then asks the parents:

- *It is now up to you and your child to decide whether to accept the offer. We will take a short break after which you can tell us what you have decided to do.*

Optional five-minute break

The refreshments should be a short distance away, and parents and child should remain in the circle with the facilitator who can provide an impartial professional view if asked (or the parents may have already decided).

During this time, the facilitator may also draft a hand-written copy of the agreement (or, if facilities are available, a printed copy). This is useful but not essential.

Reconvene

The facilitator asks the parents:

* *Please tell the meeting whether you have decided to accept the offer or not?*

Closing the conference

The facilitator will review the agreement made between the parents, the current school, and the future school/educational setting if a move has been agreed. A script is less necessary at this stage, especially since there may be many different types of agreement, and the emotional temperature should be lowered by now.

With the help of the group, finalise the agreement and then read it so that each participant is clear what part of the agreement refers to them:

* *To summarise then, (name) has agreed to (read from the agreement).*
* *(Name) has also agreed to (read from the agreement). Repeat as necessary.*
* *Is this correct?*

Check with each person.

* *Before I close the conference is there anything else anyone wants to say?*

Check with each person.

* *Thank you for attending.*

If agreement has not been reached

* *We have not reached agreement today. However, I hope that the meeting has helped you to clarify your positions and understand others better.*

Check with each person.

* *Before I close the conference is there anything else anyone wants to say?*
* *Thank you for attending.*

Good questions for the facilitator's post-conference review

* How well did I prepare the person who did the harm?
* How well did I prepare the person who was harmed?
* How well did I prepare their supporters and community member participants?

- How well did I reframe the narratives of the participants?
- How well did everyone understand the purpose and parameters of the conference?
- How well did I keep people focused on the incident?
- How well did I create an atmosphere where people felt safe to be open?
- How well did I draw out the thoughts and opinions of people in the group?
- How well did I draw out quieter people in the group?
- Was I calmly assertive with angry or disruptive people?
- Did I retain my balance when people became very emotional?
- When someone interrupted, did I calmly remind them of the ground rules so both sides were heard with respect?
- How well did I help people when they got stuck?
- How well did I empower people to speak rather than directing the group?
- How well did I help people to be creative in looking at options to repair the harm without giving them specific directions?
- How well did I help the group to develop and reach consensus?
- How well did the agreement hold accountable the person who did harm?
- How well did I support positive statements that demonstrated the value of the person who did the harm?
- Is the agreement fair, workable and specific enough?
- What can I improve or change?

Chapter 13

BECOMING A FACILITATOR

Person profile for ad-hoc facilitators

When considering who might facilitate a managed move in the absence of a trained facilitator, look for someone:

- Who is impartial and able to act with discretion.
- Whom all parties can trust and who can stimulate mutual respect.
- Who can listen empathically and enquiringly.
- Who is 'everybody's friend' and never takes sides (but is 'always on everybody's side').
- Who can act flexibly and autonomously without being unprofessional.
- Who is well-organised.

Recruiting and interviewing facilitators

The following list is designed as an aide-memoire for agencies or local authorities when preparing a person specification, job description or interview schedule for recruiting would-be facilitators. These suggestions will need to be adapted to local requirements for recruitment and the specific objectives of the recruiter.

Organisational skills to:

- Record case histories, antecedents, contexts and related data.
- Coordinate a meeting on neutral ground involving people of different ages and backgrounds.
- Record and monitor the support plan.

Communication skills to:

- Act as interlocutor, diplomat, and go-between.
- Ask the participants about their feelings, needs and requests.
- Explain things to children and families clearly.
- Use effective means of communication to share and explore sensitive issues.
- Help parents and child to revise and refine their views and statements.

- Ensure that participants at meetings are able to share their narratives, feelings and needs.
- Make explicit the feelings, needs and requests of participants, with their consent.

Interpersonal skills to:
- Understand interpersonal and group work.
- Know how to build trust rapidly.
- Creatively explore alternatives and options with children, parents, teachers and managers.
- Provide support to families and professionals.
- Guide all parties towards a common goal assertively but without coercion.
- Establish all-party consensus.
- Adopt a no-blame approach whilst making wrong-doers fully accountable.
- Work effectively with angry or frustrated people.
- Be comfortable managing awkward moments.

Knowledge and understanding of:
- Functional analysis.
- The education system and alternative options.
- The value of voluntariness and free reciprocal agreements.
- Psychological processes and systemic family theory.
- Equal opportunities, child protection and lone working policies.
- Restorative approaches and relational skills.

4

USING MANAGED MOVES ACROSS THE COMMUNITY

Chapter 14

THE EDUCATION COMMUNITY

Managed moves are best organised within a coherent community which shares a vision and philosophy. An education community should ensure that the range of learning resources and programmes it has available can meet the learning needs of *every* child, including personal, social, family and emotional development. It needs to be multi-serviced and multi-resourced, providing good value, educating effectively and meeting equal opportunities criteria.

What does an education community look like?

* An education community could comprise a small local authority, or a local authority area.
* It is likely to combine a cluster of schools (including special schools and Pupil Referral Units (PRUs)).
* It needs to be small enough for pupils to reach their place of education without excessive travel. Headteachers must be able to get to know each other and get to meetings quickly.
* The community is bound by common interests, works together for all the children under its aegis and ideally shares resources. The DCSF is committed to developing such schools partnerships.[37]
* Management of shared resources should not be onerous or bureaucratic. The community must have direct access to alternative learning resources and needs to include all other agencies and services supporting education and learning.
* Members of the community should know how and when to make use of the managed move process. There needs to be agreement about how schools and other agencies will work together to meet the requirements of all the children in that community, in a way that is fair for schools, families, children and the wider community.

---

37 http://www.teachernet.gov.uk/wholeschool/behaviour/collaboration/guidance (last accessed August 2007).

- If managed moves are to be used fairly and in a strategic way, there need to be community agreements about key issues, especially on how the future school is selected.

The boundary of inclusion

If exclusion is to be avoided, and yet children can still move from place to place within the community, we need to create a boundary of inclusion within which all children remain regardless of what they have done or what their needs are.

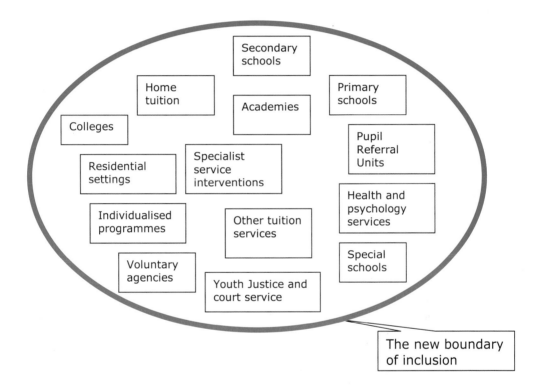

Three imperatives underpin the establishment of an education community:

Broaden schools:
- By extending teachers' skills to work with children who have substantial unmet needs, and by changing schools' culture and ethos to provide more alternatives for learning, and additional opportunities for support and development.

Build bridges:
- If children do need to move there must be a fair process for transfer – namely, managed moves.

Find a place for every child:
* There must be somewhere for the child to move to. The community must develop a range of educational opportunities to cover all learning needs, taking into account different goals and learning styles.

Sharing the burdens and rewards fairly

One question that always arises in education communities is who decides which school or agency will accept a pupil who needs a transfer. There is another question – which school can meet the needs of this child?

Some localities have developed and agreed sophisticated marking systems by which a particular school reaches the top of the 'transfer list' and receives the next pupil. This approach appears to be fair to schools, but does not take into account the needs of the pupil, or provide any element of matching or choice.

It may be more effective to have someone in the community who commands respect and trust, whose job it is to negotiate on a pupil-by-pupil basis, building good relationships with and among all the schools. This person becomes effectively 'head-teacher of all pupils not in any other school', responsible for ensuring that pupils needing additional support receive it as a coordinated package and for monitoring their progress regularly.

Funding considerations: enlightened self-interest in a boundaried community

In most local authorities the budget for alternative education is not distributed fairly, but on a first-come-first-served basis. PRUs are often full. In the absence of any cap on the number of places needed, authorities are always in danger of providing an inadequate service.

Once schools begin to work together on managing the needs of all the children in their community, they will inevitably want to start managing the alternative learning budget, and the desire to share these resources fairly will promote a new attitude. Funding strategies which enable schools to work on a real-cost basis can be devised. Each school would receive a fair share of the alternative budget and choose to spend it on- or off-site using their own learning programmes or shared ones.

The amount of money currently retained by local authorities for excluded education is considerable. If ALL of this was distributed to schools the per school share would be substantial. Schools would use these resources to pay for permanent exclusion places at real cost. Alternatively they could use them in many different ways – for instance they would be able to pool them with nearby schools to create their own alternative programmes, or put them into other community compacts and arrangements.

They could work in partnership to set up their own PRU or to buy in services from independent agencies. Those who kept pupils in school would find this cash went a very long way in paying for more staff and resources. Schools which accept children from other schools would receive funding from the excluding school at what ever level was agreed between them. In other words, if a school excludes a child, it would expect to pay the next school for the cost of their education. All sorts of possibilities arise for managed and supported moves where providers share costs, accountabilities and responsibilities.

A real-cost system would drive the total inclusion agenda of broadening schools, building bridges and finding a place for every child, because all three measures will reduce costs in ways such as these:

- When resources are shared across a community, synergies develop. For instance one school can share its Learning Support Unit (LSU) with other schools who agree to provide learning support assistants to help staff it or accept managed moves from this school.
- The local community is often underestimated. Most schools have little idea what agencies and organisations might have resources to share. Resources provided by children's charity workers, local businesses, youth volunteering networks, libraries and private tutors can add to the mix, especially when it comes to providing support for learning in the community.
- Parents and other family members can be an important resource if given sufficient support.
- Schools can pool their resources to purchase or set up provision on a shared basis.

Chapter 15

MANAGING THE CHANGE TO MANAGED MOVES IN THE EDUCATION COMMUNITY

Any group of schools that becomes an education community will have passed through a process of transformation. Change doesn't just happen, it depends on the growing awareness of the need for change, so that the harm (and hassle) of permanent exclusion can be avoided and the benefits of the alternative can be enjoyed.

A shared vision is essential – what does the 'new world' look like? Easy to grasp images and key ideas are useful, such as 'finding a place for every child somewhere within the education community'.

Above all, change depends on people who are able and willing to 'path-find' – dedicated, committed professionals who will make a personal investment in finding ways to achieve new goals.

The five key steps to transformation of the community are raising awareness, getting the big picture, developing a detailed plan, implementing it, and sustaining it.[38] The most common problem is that managers get bogged down in detailed planning, because it seems like the biggest hurdle. But fostering a climate for change and getting people on board are the things that really make the difference.

Raising awareness: consultation and the change agent's role

Some sort of consultation exercise is needed to communicate the possibilities of forming an inclusive education community, probably guided by the local authority and brokered by a 'change agent'. This external agent can play a similar role (at a community level) to that of a managed moves facilitator – bringing together the narratives of members of different interest groups and reconfiguring them into a coherent and *mutually agreeable* whole, as well as frameworking the changes of opportunity and outlook that may be required.

The change agent could be a member of a neighbouring local authority or a consultant, or the leader of one of the key agencies such as the principal educational

---

38 P. Taffinder, *Big change: A route-map for corporate transformation* (Chichester, New York, John Wiley, 1998).

psychologist. The change agent does everything that no one else has the skills and/or time to do – tasks will proliferate and the communications time-cost is very high. Their role is very substantial and yet relatively short-term. Hence the need for external resourcing – no senior manager would (or indeed should) have the capacity to do the job alongside their own.

The change agent should be a creative, lateral thinker who can write and develop visionary documents and strategic plans, and perform a diplomatic or brokering function. However, this person does not *lead* change. That role must fall to a senior member of the community, usually at assistant director level (fully supported by the Director of Children's Services).

During the process of transformation the change agent will help senior managers and other staff to identify the critical path for development, so a good deal of commitment is required from everyone. Real changes create what appear to be winners and losers with resulting friction and conflict. The leader and change agent should expect this and be ready to address and resolve issues calmly.

An effective way to carry out the consultation process is to hold two stakeholder forums – large meetings involving the key people from across the education community. Representatives of all those who may be affected by the changes, or have a contribution to make, should be invited. A small number of pupils, parents, and non-teaching staff can provide a useful 'temperature check', a sense of how it sounds to those who are managed rather than managing in the community.

At the first stakeholder forum the model for an inclusive education community (the big picture) is presented, discussed and its value-in-principle agreed. Then there is a development stage during which the change agent explores the issues with each membership group on an individual basis. The support of headteachers is crucial, in particular the support of their local champion. This is often the chair of the local association of headteachers but sometimes the leadership is on a 'first among equals' basis.

At the second forum an action plan is presented and, hopefully, agreed. If the change agent has done their work all the issues will have been raised, understood, and negotiated and solutions found to help all parties overcome their objections.

Getting the big picture

The first stakeholder forum is where the model inclusive education community and the process of managed moves are discussed. Ownership of the vision – the best incentive for action – is generated as people think through their response. At a typical forum the following key questions can be asked:

- 'How would "total inclusion" (the inclusion of all pupils within an education community within which children may change their place and style of education by a managed move) affect you?'
- 'What should happen now?'
- 'What are your feelings and thoughts about this framework, and how do you see this affecting your own needs and life-goals?'

- 'What would you need to see happen before you can be persuaded to make a commitment to total inclusion, and to convince others to do so?'

The overarching question is not 'How should we change?' or even 'What goals should we set?' but 'If we changed in particular ways to achieve particular aims, how would that affect you and how would you change your practice?'

People need to be given permission to speak their minds without fear of counter-criticism. Managers need to be primed to hear criticism without feeling defensive.

An audit of all resources, from schools to voluntary agencies, will help generate the mailing list for the stakeholder forum, and help the community appreciate the full range of local resources. The number and breadth of agencies and organisations that are available in any one locality often amazes participants. For instance, at one forum a headteacher complained about the lack of support for drugs problems and was astonished to find that a drugs support unit with a six-figure budget was based less than a mile from his school. At another, the simple act of showing participants an A4 colour graphic on which every school and agency was marked was greeted with enthusiasm. Afterwards participants said they felt an increased sense of cohesion and support.

Rural schools may find it harder to create alternative settings. However, it is not the physical location of a learning programme that matters, but the learning styles permitted, the ethos, the learning goals offered, and the type of support provided. One school could create a number of different programmes using different parts of the site or nearby locations.

The action planning stage starts after a consensus has been reached amongst heads of schools, agencies and services about the big picture, and they are receptive in principle to the proposed change of model. It's worth listening to, respecting and working to achieve a consensus with representatives of the school community, including teaching assistants, ancillary staff, unions, and also pupils and parents.

Change agents will do well to remember that people share their fears and anxieties first (often in quite defensive-aggressive ways) before sharing their needs. Collecting these is a key task at every stage because we obtain people's cooperation by meeting their needs.

Developing a detailed plan

A second round of person-to-person or small-groups consultancy now takes place amongst the people who will be responsible for the changes. This means visits to headteachers (and other key people, at all levels and in all departments) by the change agent and a local authority representative whose role is to take note of the headteachers' views and concerns. It is the change agent's job to negotiate and persuade, to calm fears and address concerns, and to build up a detailed picture about what headteachers would need to see happen before agreeing to support the changes.

Heads of agencies and services should also be consulted and their cooperation gained. But it is the headteachers who are in the pivotal position with primary responsibility for the safety and well-being of numerous children *and* the power to exclude.

The combined needs of the community drive the drafting of an action plan which reconfigures services so that they meet these needs more effectively. It is useful to circulate a copy of the draft plan and ask participants to confirm that it deals adequately with their concerns.

When this round of consultations is finished, all of the 'need to see happen' hurdles of the headteachers and others are brought together into a final action plan to expedite their cooperation.

It is time for a second stakeholder forum where the final plan can be presented to everyone involved. Some last-minute adjustments may be required and can be discussed in a collegiate way, but the plan should be approved by everyone at the forum. After all, everyone has contributed to it, and everyone has had their concerns addressed.

Senior managers heading the various local authority services and agencies will need to work together to achieve joint goals in support of education community development.

Implementation: reaching all parts of the community

A transformative process now needs to take place at grassroots level across the community. Headteachers may have agreed to establish implementation teams (a small group of managers), who will circulate teacher-training materials. New committees may be needed, or existing ones adapted to take care of key roles. In one local authority the Pupil Referral Unit (PRU) might be the focal point for managed moves, in another it might be the educational psychology service.

Above all, the education community needs to be run on economically sound lines; the number of children entering 'education otherwise than at school' needs to be about equal to the number leaving it. When the community develops more learning opportunities, more places become available. And as schools begin to offer a broader range of programmes, the load on the system is reduced. This allows the community to improve the quality of managed moves and alternative learning offers.

Conclusion

Managed moves represent a distinctly different approach to one of education's most intractable problems. It may surprise some readers to discover that enormous human potential can be unlocked when the key dynamic of voluntariness is released.

Ultimately, managed moves could replace permanent exclusion in all but a tiny number of cases. This is because exclusion is underpinned by rejection whereas managed moves are underpinned by solution-focused thinking. And as the managed move process becomes better understood, the need to act coercively will diminish.

Ethically, those with the power to make such decisions must surely attempt to arrange a managed move whenever possible rather than exclude children out of hand.

If the model proposed in this book is properly applied children will be made more accountable for their actions and be more supported in making the changes necessary when moving to a new place of learning. This 'high accountability with high support' ethic is provably the most effective means of producing positive social change – in schools and in the wider community.

On an intuitive level, the vast majority of professionals recognise that children who behave so badly or cause us so much stress also see themselves as failing, depressed and misguided. Schools are fundamentally humane organisations run by humane people. It is to be hoped that the kinder alternative will become the preferred one.

Resources

Advice on managed moves, community-based inclusion, relational skills
To contact the author, access training information and download guides:
www.inaura.net

A. Abdelnoor and P. Pisavadia, *Preliminary Assessment of Educational Managed Moves in England and Wales* (London, Inaura the inclusion charity, 2004).

Facts and figures about exclusion
A. Abdelnoor, *Preventing Exclusions* (Oxford, Heinemann (Educational), 1999).

C. Hayden and S. Dunne, *Outside, Looking In: Children's and families' experiences of exclusions from school* (London, Children's Society, 2001).

C. Parsons, *Education, Exclusion and Citizenship* (London, Routledge, 1999).

Government policy
The DCSF main portal for schools' policy on behaviour and attendance, Family and Community, and Every Child Matters:
www.teachernet.gov.uk/wholeschool/

On exclusions:
www.teachernet.gov.uk/wholeschool/behaviour/exclusion/

On managed moves:
www.teachernet.gov.uk/wholeschool/behaviour/exclusion/guidance/part1/

On school partnerships:
www.teachernet.gov.uk/wholeschool/behaviour/collaboration/guidance/

The Every Child Matters Common assessment framework:
www.everychildmatters.gov.uk

Organisational development
P. Taffinder, *Big Change: A route map for corporate transformation* (Chichester, Wiley, 1998).

Non-violent communication
The Center for Nonviolent Communication:
www.cnvc.org

M.B. Rosenberg, *Nonviolent Communication: A language of life* (California, Puddle Dancer Press, 2004).

NVC Resolutions, for information on training and resources in the UK, and global links:
www.nvc-resolutions.co.uk/nvclinks.htm

Restorative Justice
The Restorative Justice Consortium:
www.restorativejustice.org.uk

R. Graef, *Why Restorative Justice? Repairing the harm caused by crime* (London, Calouste Gulbenkian Foundation, 2001).